SINCE THE GREAT COMMISSION contains no limit on age, education or family status, either stated or implied, it becomes clear that Jesus was addressing His words of challenge and consecration to all followers of all ages."

The men and women in this book refused to let age, education, family or finances stand in the way of serving God. "All concluded, 'It's never too late to say yes to the Lord,' and their lives were revolutionized because of it."

Foreword by Cliff Barrows

Keith Brown ◆ John Hoover

It's Never Too Late to Say Yes!

Eleven inspiring
accounts of people
who made mid-
life ministry
commitments

Regal Books

A Division of GL Publications
Ventura, California, U.S.A.

Published by Regal Books
A Division of GL Publications
Ventura, California 93006
Printed in U.S.A.

Library of Congress Cataloging-in-Publication Data.

Brown, Keith. 1932-
    It's never too late to say yes : eleven inspirational accounts of people who
made mid life ministry commitments / Keith Brown with John W. Hoover
    p.   cm.
    ISBN 0-8307-1249-6
    1. Evangelists—Biography. 2.   Clergy—Biography. 3. Missionaries—
Biography. 4. Vocation, Ecclesiastical—Case studies. I. Hoover, John W.,
1950-   . II. Title.
BV3780.B69   1987   87-22179
253'.0880564—dc19   CIP

1 2 3 4 5 6 7 8 9 10 / 91 90 89 88 87

Rights for publishing this book in other languages are contracted by Gospel
Literature International (GLINT) foundation. GLINT also provides technical
help for the adaptation, translation, and publishing of Bible study resources
and books in scores of languages worldwide. For further information, contact
GLINT, Post Office Box 488, Rosemead, California, 91770, U.S.A., or the
publisher.

CONTENTS

Section One
FROM THE BUSINESS WORLD

Section Two
FROM THE MILITARY WORLD

Section Three
FROM THE ATHLETIC WORLD

Section Four
PUTTING IT TO WORK

FOREWORD
Cliff Barrows

My mother and dad illustrate perfectly what this book is all about.

Dad was a farmer and rancher in California all his life. He was active in his local church and followed my ministry with great interest and prayer. He would often go with us to crusade meetings in the United States and occasionally to our overseas crusades as well.

But when Mother and Dad retired in their mid-60s, they decided they wanted to be involved in a direct way on the mission field. Not just praying and supporting missions—as important as that is—but actually living and working on a foreign field. They simply believed no one was "too old" to be a missionary.

So they went to the Philippine Islands and served there for over four years. And what a ministry they had! Mother taught women's Bible studies in the homes and counseled countless individuals—both nationals and missionaries. She became a mother to wayward children off the street and welcomed them into her home, sharing and teaching about Jesus' love for them.

Dad drew on all his farming knowledge and experience. He helped a school develop its own breeding stock of chicks so the school could support itself; he planned and oversaw construction of a new road into a remote area of the Philippines; he developed an experimental farm to help Filipinos learn better production methods. In addition, Dad had an exciting ministry showing gospel films in schools, prisons, and town plazas all over the Islands. He was greatly used of God to stir the Gideons organization to do more in the Philippines than they had ever done before.

Take it from Dad and Mother Barrows. No one is ever too old to be used by God in some part of His harvest field. Just give Him a person who has unlimited availability to Him—even one with limited formal education and limited stamina—though you could never convince me that advanced age necessarily translates into reduced ability, judging from Mother and Dad's boundless energy.

The stories you are about to read are all about real people. Ordinary people just like Mother and Dad, used by God in an extraordinary way as they obediently followed God's leading in their lives. May their tribe increase, and may you become a part of that tribe.

Cliff Barrows
The Billy Graham Evangelistic Association

AN INTRODUCTION DESIGNED TO BE READ

The context may vary, but the comments are disturbingly familiar:

- A pastor prays, "Lord, lay your hand on *some of our young people* here tonight. Raise up many from our *high school and college group* who still have their whole lives before them, and call them to serve you . . . . "

- A conference speaker closes the final service with this challenge: "I want all of you *teenagers* who feel the Lord calling you into full-time service to come forward . . . . "

- A poster advertising World Missions Awareness Day proclaims: "The world needs missionaries, and World Missions Day provides a special one-hour program about foreign mission service. Although it will be of great interest to all the members of our church, it has been especially created to inform our *young men and women* about the opportunities they have to become overseas missionaries after they graduate from college."

• A radio pastor, after interviewing a veteran missionary, comments, "We have a tape available of this special program. Perhaps you would like to obtain a copy to share with a *young couple* you know who might be thinking about missions."

• A church bulletin carries a lead article entitled "On Becoming a World Christian," which states: "It is . . . exciting to see God's Spirit touching the lives of many of our *young people* today and witnessing their response in saying, 'Yes, send me.'"

• A write-up following an enormously successful missions conference captures this highlight: "It was thrilling to see the great crowd of *young people* who surged to their feet all over the auditorium to give themselves for missions . . . between 600 and 800 *under 30 years of age* . . . just exploding down the aisles."

• A sincere church member, speaking to a 50-year-old man on the occasion of his departure for a first term of service in Africa, is heard to remark: "The people in our church really like you and your family, and appreciate your ministry. I'm sure the church would support you if only you had *graduated from seminary* and were *younger.*"

To all of these appeals and comments which I have personally heard or read, I want to cry out, "Hold it! Stop! Wait a minute! Where did you find *that* in the Bible?" Is my

Bible only an abridgment of yours?

Have I perhaps overlooked a conditional clause in Matthew 28:19? "Go into all the world—all you who are under forty—and make disciples of all nations."

Is there perhaps a rendering of Luke 24:48 I have failed to notice? "You are witnesses of these things—all you young people with your whole lives before you."

Did the apostle John in 20:21 omit something when he quoted our Lord? "As the Father has sent me, even so I am sending you—all of you who are unencumbered by middle-age years and large-size families."

Has something been overlooked in the marching orders Jesus left for His disciples? "You shall be my witnesses to the ends of the earth—all you healthy, robust recent graduates from Bible school or seminary."

What do these obvious parodies of actual Scripture tell us? Simply this: Since the Great Commission contains no such limit on age, education or family status, either stated or implied, it becomes clear that Jesus was addressing His words of challenge and consecration to all followers of all ages.

That's not to say there's no place for young people in missions today.

In fact, my personal experience contradicts nearly everything you're about to read in this book. I did it the "usual" way—some would say the "right" way. College, seminary, deputation and straight to the mission field, all by the age of 26. My wife was 23.

That was the "right" way back then. In fact, it was practically the only way. Until fairly recently, most mission boards wouldn't look twice at an application from a man over 40. "Too old to learn a language," the personnel director would say. "Not enough flexibility to adjust to a foreign culture. He's got a wife and how many children?

Seems qualified in his profession, but it has no relationship to what we're doing. No theological training, either."

David Howard has written an excellent book entitled *Student Power*. In it he documents how the last century of world missions has been largely initiated and sustained by students. The facts speak eloquently for the considerable—and continuing—role for those in their teens and twenties in fulfilling the Great Commission.

But a new wind is blowing. A new wave of mission impetus is growing. Call it "Middle-age Power." New missionaries walking on older legs.

Mid-life career changes are common today, and the motivations behind them are surprisingly varied: larger salary, potential for advancement, a change of scenery or climate, health or family considerations.

The men and women you will meet in the following chapters all have one thing in common: a significant change of career at an unlikely time of life. But their motivation was not money, escape from boredom or desire for advancement. Rather, their hearts burned with a passion best summarized in the words of the apostle Paul: "Woe is unto me, if I preach not the gospel" (1 Cor. 9:16, *KJV*).

In a variety of exciting and often unexpected ways, God has divinely guided and redirected their lives into channels of service which at first glance might appear improbable, if not impossible. They discovered there's more than a modicum of truth to the adage, "Life begins at 40"—especially life in the service of the King.

A nonagenarian was asked, "What does it feel like to be 90 years of age?" After a moment's reflection he answered, "Well, at least I don't have to worry too much about peer pressure." Growing older does not have to be synonymous with diminished mental, physical or spiritual activity and usefulness, as these examples illustrate:

- Grandma Moses took up painting when she was in her 70s, and continued well past her hundredth birthday, fashioning over 500 celebrated works of art.

- Golda Meir was 71 when she became prime minister of Israel.

- George Bernard Shaw was 94 when one of his plays was first produced.

- Benjamin Franklin helped to frame the Constitution of the United States at the age of 81.

- Edna Whyte was 67 when she designed and built an airport that accommodates 350 planes. Today at 81, she still flies four to six hours a day, competes in air races three times a year, and performs as an aerobatic stunt pilot.

The Peace Corps knows the value of "salt and pepper" wisdom. One of their advertisements reads: "For some people, retirement doesn't mean taking it easy. Today's Peace Corps is for *anyone* who has experience they would like to share where it's needed—no matter how old you are." That challenge encouraged Mrs. Lillian Carter, mother of former President Jimmy Carter, to travel to India at age 68.

An advertisement for full-time Christian workers today might well read: "Wanted: Volunteers for the Prince of Peace Corps. Open to all Christians who have experience to share where it's needed—no matter how old you are."

There is ample biblical support for such an "ageless" appeal:

- Noah was 500 years old when he started a new career as a shipbuilder. After his watery adventure in the Flood, Noah lived to be 950 years old. Thus he was past the midpoint of his life when he changed careers.
- Caleb was 85 years old when he told General Joshua, "Give me this mountain" (Josh. 14:12, *KJV*), knowing it would take a strength beyond his own to rid it of its giant inhabitants.
- Abraham was 75 when God chose him to move in a new direction—both geographically and spiritually.
- Moses was 80 when God redirected his life from the unlikely "podium" of a burning bush.
- Joshua was at least 70 when Moses commissioned him to take over the leadership role in the nation of Israel.
- The greatest missionary of the New Testament period—the apostle Paul—was likely in his mid-40s when he launched his missionary career.

Their tribe continues to increase today in the person of Arthur Lown, blind missionary to the Philippines; Bob Waymire, aerospace engineer turned global strategist; Paul Neumann, professional basketball player turned Bible teacher; and eight others you will meet in these pages. All are men and women who refused to let age, education, family or finances stand in the way of serving God. And all concluded, "It's never too late to say yes to the Lord," and their lives were revolutionized because of it.

Just imagine how differently your own life story might read if you come to that same transforming conclusion.

Section One
FROM THE BUSINESS WORLD

1

THE SAILOR WHO FORGOT HIS DATE

Dick and Frances Harris

"Dick, you have two choices: come back home or divorce."

Heading off to seminary ought to be a happy time. But for 45-year-old Dick Harris, it was turning into a nightmare.

Excitedly, he had shared with his wife Frances that God had called him into the ministry. He could scarcely have been prepared for her angry response. She announced that God had not spoken to her, and flatly refused to go with him.

Two days later as Dick drove away, his wife's last words were still ringing in his ears: "Deserter . . . louse . . . bum."

What could possibly make a successful middle-aged businessman leave behind the "good life" and go off to seminary over the protests of his wife?

Dick Harris's mother gave her son this advice early in

life: "Get a good education, make a lot of money, and then you'll be happy." The advice was deeply rooted in the family's unhappy past.

Dick grew up during the Great Depression. His father had difficulty finding work, leading to the loss of the family home and a steady succession of moves. Although Dick's parents were not particularly religious, they did send Dick and his sister to Sunday School. Dick heard a steady stream of Christian talk, but the words rang hollow.

Commenting about that period in his life, Dick said: "The phrase 'stop the world, I want to get off' had not yet been coined. But if it had, I would have claimed it as my own because I had so much unhappiness."

Happiness Is . . .

Dick's mother talked to her son often about the elusive goal of happiness. Her father was uneducated, and, by her own admission, "we were never happy." But that only served to rekindle her desire to bring happiness to her son.

During junior and senior high school, Dick started saving toward his college education. He arose early to deliver papers, and worked late after school doing odd jobs. Enrolling in the University of Miami, Dick started to get his future together. Education, money, happiness—his mother would have been proud. But then came December 7, 1941—Pearl Harbor—and within a few weeks Dick had joined the navy.

After boot camp Dick received his orders to go overseas. His destination: a hotspot of fighting. For the first time Dick began to think, "This is getting serious! What if I go overseas and someone shoots me and I die. Then I'll never be happy. And what will happen to me then?"

Dick began to search for the meaning of life beyond the grave. He asked himself, Would I go to heaven if I died? The answer that came back was anything but reassuring. Then would I go to hell? From what he had heard about the place, he certainly had no desire to go there.

He continued his personal investigation and thought of a third option: Maybe I could just go out in limbo somewhere, into nothingness. But that possibility too lacked appeal.

The Strong Arm of an Elder

Just prior to shipping out, Dick had a few days of home leave. What better way to go, he reasoned, than to get a date and have one last fling.

Dick remembered a girl he had dated a few times in high school. As he started to call her Sunday morning, he remembered that her family always went to church. Fearing that someone else might ask her if he waited until that afternoon, Dick dressed up and went to church himself. He planned only to make sure she was there and then wait outside until the service was over. As Dick was peeking in the back door, an elder from the church came up behind him, took him by the arm, and ushered him to a seat.

Inwardly, Dick seethed. He hadn't intended to go to church. But the minister's first words riveted his attention: "The Bible was written so that a person could know that when he died, he would go to heaven."

Dick sat straight up in his seat. He thought to himself, "This man sounds like he has the answer to my problems. I'd better listen to him." By the time the sermon was finished, Dick had accepted Jesus Christ as his Savior. During the invitation he responded by making a public declaration of his decision.

Date? What Date?

Dick had found the happiness which so long he had sought. Overjoyed by his new relationship with the Lord, he completely forgot about his date—which, for a sailor about to ship out, must have been a first!

During the two-mile walk home, he began thinking that he would like to do something for God to demonstrate his appreciation. Dick recalls, "The thought came to me that I could give up something. So I decided to give up swearing. During the six months in the navy, my vocabulary had increased sizeably. So I made a covenant with God right then and there that I would stop swearing. And for over 40 years I have kept that covenant."

Dick goes on to say with a smile, "Maybe I should have given up some other things too!"

George Must Be in Heaven

During his time in the navy, Dick could find little in the way of Christian fellowship or discipleship training. He recalled his disastrous first attempt at witnessing: "I was sitting on my bunk reading the New Testament my pastor had given me. Three buddies came by and began ridiculing me for reading the Bible. All I could think to say was, 'Where do you think George Washington is?' My thought process at that moment was something like this: George Washington was one of the greatest men I knew; great men go to heaven; so certainly George must be in heaven."

Dick's buddies went on their way doubled over with laughter.

While still in the navy, Dick met and married Frances. After his discharge they moved to Miami. Recalling his mother's advice to "get an education, make lots of money, and find happiness," Dick launched into a new career. His life values were still rooted in the world system. Jesus was his Savior; but Dick was his own master. And now more than ever, Dick wanted to provide the material things of the world for his wife and children—"so they could all be happy."

After graduation from the University of Miami, Dick started working in the title insurance and abstract business. Driving himself to become successful, he found his work consuming more and more of his time. Eventually it paid off as he was elected president of his company—a remarkable accomplishment since he was not even a stockholder!

Active in civic affairs, Dick soon became president of the Junior Chamber of Commerce, as well as the chamber's state vice president and national director. He was encouraged by many of his associates to run for mayor of Fort Lauderdale. Turning that down, he did become campaign manager for a U.S. congressman, a governor, and a state senator.

Dick had fulfilled two-thirds of his mother's advice. He was educated, he was making lots of money, but he hadn't found happiness. He invested heavily in real estate in the Cape Canaveral area of Florida. His personal assets were in excess of $1 million. He was living what many would call the "good life": a beautiful home, country club surroundings, Cadillacs and Thunderbirds to drive, a 32-foot Chris Craft boat for leisure moments.

Through all of this, Dick remained active in church affairs. He became a charter member of a new church in Fort Lauderdale—Coral Ridge Presbyterian Church— which had issued a call to a young pastor, D. James Kennedy, just out of seminary. Could either man have envisaged then that that same church was destined to become one of the largest in the state of Florida with that same young student fresh out of seminary, now Dr. D. James Kennedy, still its pastor?

They Said "Go Forth" So We Went

Something happened in that small, struggling church that changed the entire direction of Dick's life. Dr. Kennedy began to teach laypeople how to share their faith. Dick was among the first group of eight to receive the training—the forerunner of what would later become "Evangelism Explosion."

At the end of the 12-week training period, Dr. Kennedy said, "Okay, now go out and witness." Dick recalls, "We did go out. But we all went home."

Clearly something was missing in the training program. The group was given an additional 12 weeks of training. Again they were told, "Go out." And again, as before, they went home.

Dick explains what went wrong by saying, "No one likes to fail. We didn't witness because we had never done it before. The risk of failure was just too great."

Finally one evening, Dr. Kennedy pulled Dick aside. "I want you to go with me tonight."

Dick asked, "Where are we going?"

"Witnessing," was the terse reply.

Dick immediately began to think of many reasons why he couldn't go. But Dr. Kennedy's instructions caught him up short: "I only want you to do one thing, Dick. I want you to go with me and promise you won't say a word. Just sit there."

Dick couldn't believe his ears. Surely this was one assignment he could not fail!

That night they visited a couple and their teenage daughter. At the close of Dr. Kennedy's gospel presentation, all three trusted Christ as their Savior.

In thinking back to that pivotal experience, Dick reflects: "It was the most thrilling thing I had ever seen. Everything Dr. Kennedy taught us worked."

The following week they went again, with Dr. Kennedy talking and Dick praying. Finally, after many evenings together, Dick said to Dr. Kennedy, "Look, tonight you sit there quietly and let me do the talking. And if I goof it up, you jump in and straighten it out." Which, of course, is exactly what Dr. Kennedy had been hoping would happen all along! Dick shared and God blessed. A new zeal was awakening in Dick to see men and women come to Christ.

The President Changes Things

Politics has a way of bringing sudden changes and, in the process, changing the course of many lives. Lyndon Johnson, only three months after being sworn in as president, decided to transfer much of the space agency from Cape Canaveral, Florida to Houston, Texas. Overnight, Dick's large investments in the Cape Canaveral region were practically worthless.

But Dick's business woes were not over yet. A wholesale nursery company he had invested in went through a drought and two hurricanes. The few palm trees and plants that survived the dry weather were flattened by the high winds. Suddenly, Dick the millionaire found himself broke and out of a job.

Occasionally, one of Dick's Christian friends would ask him, "Have you ever thought about going into the ministry? With your gift of evangelism and your ability to teach the Bible, it seems right that you should be in the ministry."

Dick would counter with a ready list of excuses: "Look, I'm 45 years old. I have a wife and three sons—one in high school, one in college, and one about to enter college. Besides, if God had wanted me in the ministry, He would have arranged things that way. I'd have gone to a Bible college, married the daughter of a missionary, gone to seminary, and become a pastor." To Dick, it didn't make sense any other way.

Strawberries, Cantaloupes and Cucumbers

Dick returned to his business pursuits. He reasoned, "I came from nothing to become a millionaire; I can do it again."

He learned of an exciting new farming venture in the Dominican Republic. After raising a million dollars to get started, he planted 500 acres of strawberries. The result was gorgeous plants—but no berries.

So Dick turned his interests to cantaloupe. Although the plants produced delicious melons, the fruit had a disturbing habit of turning black within three hours after being taken out of refrigeration. And whoever heard of buying a black cantaloupe?

A third attempt at farming, this time for cucumbers, proved equally unsuccessful. Just as the harvest came in, the bottom dropped out of the cucumber market and Dick had no place to sell his produce. This last debacle ended Dick's brief farming career.

"But the song says, 'Three strikes you're out,'"[1] Dick consoled himself, "and I had only struck out twice—once at the Cape and once in the Dominican Republic." So he

If I had stayed in business with the company in Florida, I would be making in excess of $100,000 a year. Would I trade it now? I wouldn't trade it for 100 times $100,000. Not for anything would I trade."

—Dick Harris

went "back to bat" once more—this time in the lumber business. The day before Dick was to sign a contract paying him a handsome salary, 10 percent of the profits, and 10 percent ownership in the company, the owner called to tell Dick he had decided instead to sell the operation to another company.

A Three-word Prayer

Two days later, a Sunday, Dick attended his usual 6:30 A.M. prayer meeting with some of the church leaders. But he confesses his thoughts were not on the Sunday services. "All of a sudden, I was overwhelmed with the thought that Monday morning I would have nothing. No money. No job prospect. Nothing."

As Dick thought deeply about the direction of his life, the Holy Spirit began to show him a dimension that had been largely neglected. Dick knew Jesus Christ as his Savior; now he wanted Him more than ever to be Lord of his life.

In the past there had always been strings attached: "Jesus, I want you to be Lord of my life *if* . . . you bless my business ventures; *if* . . . you get me through this tough time." But that morning, Dick prayed the shortest, simplest prayer of his life: "Lord, use me."

I Want You to Do Me a Favor

Later that afternoon a friend named Virginia visited the Harris home. During the conversation, she asked, "Dick, why don't you go into the ministry?"

Dick gave his well-rehearsed reply: "Virginia, that's impossible. I'm 45 years old, I have a wife and three sons, and I'm broke."

Virginia continued, "How much money would it take?"

Dick replied, "I really don't know. Maybe with some scholarship help, $4,500 a year minimum."

That evening after the church service, Dick was walking across the parking lot with his friend, Charlie. Their usual light conversation took a serious turn.

"Dick, I want you to do me a favor."

"What's that, Charlie?"

"I want you to go to seminary for me. I don't have the education, but you do. And I want to help you. You'll recall that five years ago my wife left me. I've prayed all this time that we could work things out. But it's apparent now that we can't. So I have filed for divorce. All this time I've been sending her $600 a month. Now I won't be doing that any more. Dick, I want you to take that $600 a month and go to seminary."

At home later that evening, Dick reviewed the day's amazing events. Snatches of conversation came back to him: "Virginia, I don't know. Maybe $4,500." "Dick, I want you to use that $600 a month and go to seminary."

"Is God really able to supply all my needs out of His riches in glory?" Dick mused.

What, Pray Tell, Is a Seminary?

Dick could hardly sleep that night. The next morning he went to talk to his pastor. "Dr. Kennedy, do you know what Charlie wants me to do? I can't accept that money from him."

Dr. Kennedy answered, "Dick, I know you believe the Bible. What about the verse that says it's more blessed to give than to receive? Would you want to deny Charlie the blessing that God has for him? And besides, the church will give you $100 a month. That makes $700. You can make it on that."

After a long pause, Dick responded, "Doc, what's a seminary and where do I find one?"

Dr. Kennedy picked up the phone and called Reformed Seminary in Jackson, Mississippi. Although classes had already been in session for three weeks, if Dick could be there by Friday he could enroll.

As he hung up the phone, Dr. Kennedy said, "Dick, you can go. But let me ask you one thing first. Is there anything else you can do?"

"There is nothing else I can do," Dick answered honestly.

"Okay then, go. Too many men make the mistake of going into the ministry when they are not called of God. But Dick, I believe you are called."

They Shoot Deserters, Don't They?

The money situation was cared for. Dick could enroll if he got to Jackson by Friday. It was now Monday. But what about his three sons? And his dear wife, Frances? She had stayed close by his side through all his ups and downs. What would she say to this new direction in his life?

His three sons were thrilled. They knew this was what their dad wanted to do, and they were behind him 100 percent.

When Dick talked to Frances, it was a different story. He told her how God had called him into the ministry. Frances responded cooly, "That's fine. But I haven't heard a word. God is not calling me to the ministry. I won't go."

Two days later, Wednesday, as Dick was leaving for the airport, he left Francis standing in the middle of the living room floor, crying and accusing him of desertion. It was not the "send off" he had hoped for.

Dick's first class at Reformed did little to lift his spirits.

It was a language course—Hebrew, to be exact. Dick recalls, "It had taken me four years to complete a regular two-year Spanish class in high school. Now this. And to add to my troubles, the class was already three weeks ahead of me since I had enrolled late." When that first class mercifully drew to a close, Dick walked out, looked up to heaven, and told the Lord, "See, God. I knew I was right. I don't belong here."

A Tale of Two Choices

Two weeks passed, and Frances called. It was not a pleasant conversation as she sternly announced, "You have two choices. One, come back home. Two, a divorce."

"Listen, Fran," Dick pleaded, "a phone is a lousy place to talk about a divorce. Wait till I get home for Thanksgiving and we'll talk about it then." Frances agreed to wait.

When Dick arrived home, they talked. "Fran, I only ask two things of you. One, that you be my wife. Two, that you be the mother of my boys."

Frances replied, "You mean I don't have to be involved with those kookie people over at the seminary?"

"No."

"And will I have to go to church?"

"Not if you don't want to."

"Well, I've been your wife, and I've been mother to those three boys. I guess I can do that."

Christmas was moving day. As the months went by, God graciously and lovingly dealt with Frances. By the time the three years were over, she had worked in that "kookie" seminary, first in the library and later in leadership roles with the women's groups. Today, she remains Dick's helpmeet and a strongly devoted, thoroughly supportive minister's wife.

First Prize—or Booby Prize?

It wasn't always financially easy during those days, what with Dad in seminary and two sons in college. Dick and Fran went grocery shopping every Friday evening. But one Friday, they found they had no food in the house, and no money to buy any food.

As they prayed about their problem, the telephone rang. The voice on the other end belonged to the grocery store manager: "Congratulations, you have won first prize in our drawing. Come right down and claim your prize."

God's timing could not have been more perfect! Dick and Fran wept with joy. Now they would have food to eat. But they were about to learn another lesson in God's manifold ways of supplying the needs of His children.

The store manager proudly presented them with a beautiful silver set—complete with platter, tea and coffee pots, creamer, and sugar bowl.

Back home, admiring their new silver service through their tears, Dick and Fran heard the door bell ring. It was an insurance salesman friend of Dick's, who entered hesitantly and apologized profusely. "A few years back I readjusted your insurance policies. I said at the time I was doing it for you. But actually, I adjusted them so I would benefit by receiving a bigger commission. The Lord hasn't given me a moment's peace about it. I've got to make restitution. So here," and he thrust a check for $821 into Dick's hand.

After the salesman left, Fran decided that the Lord must have a great sense of humor. She has since concluded that if her house should ever start to burn and she could only save one item, it would be the silver service, which will always be a daily reminder of God's faithfulness and provision.

After graduating from seminary at age 48, Dick served for three years as associate pastor for evangelism at the First Presbyterian Church in Jackson, Mississippi, and later as associate pastor at the First Presbyterian Church in Chattanooga, Tennessee. Then for over 10 years Dick served as the senior pastor at the Wayside Presbyterian Church in Signal Mountain, Tennessee, where he led an active, missions-minded congregation.

During those years Dick's burden for missions increased. "I just wasn't content with having a missions conference once a year," Dick said. As well as having many missionaries come to the church to speak about their ministry around the world, Dick made several personal trips himself to visit missionaries on the field.

It's not surprising, then, to know that almost the next week after Dick retired recently from pastoring, he began his current ministry with Wycliffe Bible Translators. He is now their representative for the state of Mississippi. Dick's new ministry takes him all over the state telling people about the important work of Wycliffe. He's always on the lookout for people who are interested, not only in financially supporting the work of missions, but going themselves as missionaries.

A Final Thought

I asked Dick if he ever had any regrets about his life since making his career change. He said with a twinkle in his eye, "Just a few days ago I was talking with a young man in my congregation who has become very successful. I was sharing with him a little of my background in business. I told him if I had stayed in business with the company in Florida, I would be making in excess of $100,000 a year. He asked me the same question—would I trade it now? I told him I wouldn't trade it for 100 times $100,000."

"Now," Dick went on, "I'll be honest with you. There are times occasionally when I think back to what I had at one point in my life. I must say I did enjoy that Chris Craft boat and those trips over to the Bahamas. And I enjoyed living on that golf course. I enjoyed walking down the streets and having everyone know me and speak to me as someone important and successful. Yes, I have those thoughts occasionally. But they are fleeting thoughts.

"When it comes down to the serious business of my life, there are no regrets. Not for anything would I trade. Just looking at my congregation on Sunday and seeing all the people who have come to know the Lord, and those who are maturing in the Lord spiritually, makes it all worthwhile. And now, having the privilege of representing a fine mission organization like Wycliffe has added a new and exciting dimension to my life. No, I wouldn't trade it for anything in the world."

When Dick Harris makes a statement like that, even E. F. Hutton listens.

Note

1. From Jack Norworth's "Take Me Out to the Ball Game." Public domain.

2

CALLING A BLIND MAN'S BLUFF

Arthur and Inez Lown

Pretend for a moment you are the personnel manager for a large corporation. Two candidates present themselves for a job opening. Candidate A was a 4.0 student in school, has three degrees—bachelor's, master's, doctorate—and a wealth of on-the-job experience. Candidate B is blind, 48 years old and has a large family.

Question: Which candidate gets the job?

Answer: Take your pick. They're both the same individual!

One Sunday night after church, I invited Arthur Lown and his family over for a snack and a time of fellowship. He said they would be delighted to come, and asked for directions. I narrated the rather complicated series of streets, stop lights, and turns necessary to find our house in northeast suburban Atlanta. He repeated the directions back to me word for word, as if reading off a map, then found our house without one wrong turn.

Suddenly it struck me. Arthur Lown is blind. No, he did not drive that night. But then, as you'll learn by reading his remarkable story, Arthur has been making people forget he's blind for most of his life.

When anyone leaves the comfortable surroundings of home to head overseas as a cross-cultural missionary, it's exciting news. But add to that the "barriers" of someone approaching 50 years of age with three children and no sight, and you have the tale of Arthur Lown, the man who never learned the meaning of the word *handicapped*.

Arthur was born in Lexington, South Carolina, the youngest of four children. His father was a carpenter, his mother a school teacher. From birth, Arthur was diagnosed as having a distortion of the retina called retinitis pigmentosa—a disease for which there is no known cure. As a child, he was able to distinguish between shades of gray, seeing "men as trees, walking" (Mark 8:24, *KJV*) but could not identify people by sight.

Arthur's mother began teaching her nearly sightless son at home in the first grade. At the age of eight, he entered a state school for the deaf and blind, where he received the rest of his elementary and secondary education. If Arthur's blindness was supposed to be a childhood handicap, no one bothered to tell him. He learned to play the piano and violin, and graduated with a straight *A* average.

Pardon My Inconvenience

Even today Arthur is very open about his blindness. "All my life, blindness has been an inconvenience—a burden, if you will. When I was younger I was envious of other young people who seemed to have a winsome personality. They could make friends a lot easier than I could. I was usually lonely even in a group. At times, I would gladly have traded my intellectual ability for the fun of being able to live as a 'normal' person.

"I was constantly striving to do something that counted, something that was significant, in order to compensate for my blindness. And even now, I have flashes of resentment, when I have to ride public transportation instead of driving my own car, when I can't tell which way the light switch goes in order to turn the lights on or off."

After Arthur graduated from high school, he was awarded a one-year scholarship to study Ediphone Transcription at Watertown, Massachusetts. There he learned braille, shorthand, and typing, with the thought of working as a civil service secretary.

But Arthur wasn't content with that. He went on to the University of South Carolina and received a bachelor's degree in sociology and English. Next a master's degree in education.

Then two years in seminary to prepare himself for teaching braille and theology in China. That door closed with the coming of the Communists—and probably just as well for Arthur. For though he was an expert in braille, he knew precious little about theology. In fact, by his own admission he wasn't even a believer at the time.

Years earlier Arthur had attended church. But he admits, "The thing I enjoyed most about church when I was young was going with my mother on Saturday to a ladies' group. I knew if I was patient enough, the refreshments would be worth the wait."

After finishing his formal education, Arthur took a job in the Atlanta public school system. There he provided instruction in braille, coached blind students in their regular school subjects, acted as liaison between the blind students and their parents and teachers, and supervised the preparation of equivalent textbooks in braille. In addition, he worked to change the classroom policy regarding blind students, so that they could be integrated into regular classes rather than isolated in classes of their own.

A Fireman Starts a Fire

Arthur continued to attend church occasionally, mostly to be entertained and to break up the monotony of his weekly routine. His first genuine interest in the Bible and spiritual things came at the age of 30. Arthur's next-door neighbor, a city fireman, frequently spent time with him. The fireman took every opportunity to relate daily life happenings to Scripture.

Arthur recalls, "The new meaning which he showed me from various passages was so appealing that I went with him to church. One day I heard a sermon on Jeremiah 10:23 (*NKJV*): 'O Lord, I know the way of man is not in himself; It is not in man who walks to direct his own steps.' From that time on I began to search the Bible in earnest. Though all my life I had known *about* Jesus, from that message I *met* Jesus personally."

Arthur's newfound faith in a living Christ also helped him see his blindness from God's perspective. "Having observed God's unspeakable love for me, I could now trust Him to do all things well, regardless of how things appeared.

"It is natural to ask why? But immediately the answer comes from the lips of Jesus Himself. When a man who was born blind was brought to Jesus, He answered the disciples' question, 'Neither this man nor his parents sinned,

If an all-knowing God made me to be blind, certainly I can trust His purpose and power to help me through my blindness. And it's all right. Not because I am so great in overcoming it, but because I can trust God."

—Arthur Lown

but that the works of God should be revealed in him' (John 9:3, *NKJV*). If I were not blind, then the example of God's ability to provide for me in spite of blindness would not be visible to others to cause them to marvel at God's greatness.

"Another verse that has been helpful is Exodus 4:11 (*NKJV*): 'So the Lord said to him, "Who made man's mouth? Or who makes the mute, the deaf, the seeing, or the blind? Have not I, the Lord?"' I saw in this verse that the Lord Himself takes the responsibility for making people blind. If an all-knowing God made me to be blind, certainly I can trust His purpose and power to help me through my blindness. And it's all right. Not because I am so great in overcoming it, but because I can trust God.

"It's like viewing a tapestry. If you look at it up close, all you see is individual threads and snatches of design. But if you move back, you can see the tapestry as a total creation. If I just focus on my blindness it's not a pretty picture. But when I move back to view the whole work of God and see things from His perspective, I can rest in the fact that God does all things well."

It Pays to Advertise

As Arthur continued his work in Atlanta, he felt the growing need for more training. Taking a leave of absence, he went to Columbia University in New York, where he received his doctorate in administration and special education. Returning to Atlanta, he became the administrator of the supportive services program for blind students in Atlanta and eight other neighboring school systems. Because of his impressive credentials, he was asked to serve on several national education boards, as well as to speak on the university lecture circuit.

Something else happened while Arthur was at Columbia. "It occurred to me that I was still single and 34 years old. Up until then, each girl I had dated was either unacceptable to me, or I to her. For the first time in my life I committed the matter directly to God, believing that He would do the best for me—whether that best was to remain single or be married.

"I had posted a notice on the bulletin board at the university, advertising for a reader to help me with my studies. One who answered the notice was Inez. It didn't take long to recognize that each was the answer to the other's prayers. Inez said she too had prayed for guidance in selecting a husband if the Lord so desired. We were married later that year."

Two Thousand Tongues to Go

Arthur and Inez's lives began to turn in an exciting new direction. In 1960, they read a book entitled *Two Thousand Tongues to Go*, the story of Wycliffe Bible Translators (WBT). This was the Lowns' first exposure to world missions. They contacted the Wycliffe area director in Atlanta and began meeting some WBT missionaries. Arthur was impressed with their dedication and the personal interest they took in his family. Becoming active with Wycliffe in a lay capacity, Arthur and Inez were soon arranging film showings in churches, distributing literature, transporting and housing missionaries, and praying for the expanding work of Wycliffe worldwide.

Before long, another step of commitment followed. At a banquet in which Wycliffe's work was presented, Arthur and Inez were challenged to support the ministry through a faith promise, stretching themselves beyond their known sources of income, and trusting God to enable them to give more. Inez read the amounts listed on the commitment card: $24 for the year, $60, $120, $240, up to a top figure of $1,200 for the year.

"Check the $1,200 box, Inez," Arthur said.

Understandably, Inez was nervous. "Do you really know what you are doing?"

"Yes I do," he replied. "God will enable us to meet that $1,200 faith promise. Please check it." Inez did—with reservations.

Because Arthur was a teacher, his summer months were mostly free. That summer, for the first time in his teaching career, he was called by the library for the blind, offering him part-time summer employment. His income: $1,250—just enough to meet his faith promise and pay his busfare back and forth to the library for the entire summer.

The next year the Lowns doubled their faith promise. The year following, they doubled it again. Each year the Lord enabled them to meet their commitment by giving Arthur a promotion or a raise. This remarkable series of answered prayers, faith commitments and faithful provisions from the Lord finally persuaded Arthur to investigate career opportunities with Wycliffe.

"I had never observed any ability in myself to transform people. But it was easy to imagine myself as a vessel, a carrier, an instrument through whom the Word itself would do the work of transformation.

"I was convinced of the truth of Isaiah 55, that God's Word was powerful and would not return empty if we sowed it. It was easy to see myself as part of the mechanism to help make this Word available to those who had never heard. The question for me was whether I personally had any contribution to make beyond representing WBT here at home."

Putting It to the Test

Wycliffe was much interested in a man of Arthur's education and experience. They were impressed with his dedication and commitment to missions. But after all, he *did* have that "handicap"—blindness. Could he actually function in a foreign environment where there are no sidewalks, no crosswalks and where crowds of people give way to no one? And even if he could cope with life on the mission field, what kind of job could a sightless missionary perform?

In order to test the waters, Arthur and Inez spent a week touring Wycliffe's work in Mexico. Later that same year, the Lowns traveled to a Wycliffe base in Colombia, South America, where for six weeks Arthur learned to operate the radio system. That trip proved to his satisfaction—and Wycliffe's—that he could indeed function successfully in a foreign country.

Arthur returned home from Colombia more committed than ever to become a missionary. "Year by year the work of administering the education of blind children in Atlanta, as important as it was, began to pale by comparison with the desire to bring light to those living in spiritual darkness. I was moved by the conviction that not everyone has the same opportunity to hear. My conscience would not let me continue helping the blind in Atlanta—a secure position which many others were qualified to hold and eager to fill—while far more needy, sighted persons outside the United States beckoned from their spiritual darkness."

Manila Calling Dr. Lown

John Kyle, long-time friend working with Wycliffe in the Philippines, called to ask if Arthur would consider coming to fill a vacancy as administrator of the center in Manila. Inez would be in charge of the Wycliffe guest house.

"Inez was very supportive during the whole decision-making process," Arthur recalls. "In fact, before we were married she had planned to go to Africa as a nurse. So the decision for her was very easy. And for me, all the various components had come together as well. We had no doubt in our mind the direction the Lord was taking us."

And so, two years shy of his fiftieth birthday, Arthur began his missionary career in Manila, Philippines, even though in the opinion of many he was too old, too handicapped to serve the Lord effectively and too "encumbered" with a wife and two children.

Initially, the Lowns went to Manila as short-term assistants (STAs), planning to stay for a maximum of two years. But the more they became involved in the ministry of Wycliffe, the longer stretched their "short-term" assignment.

It would be six years before the Lowns returned home to Atlanta. When they did, Arthur discovered certain state laws governing the teaching profession had been changed. Having resigned as a 23-year veteran teacher, Arthur still did not qualify for a pension. But with the revision in the laws, Arthur learned he would be eligible for retirement after just two more years in the classroom. The Atlanta school system was hiring no new teachers at the time, yet Arthur was rehired.

The Blind Leading the Sighted

Two years later, Arthur and his family returned to Manila to continue their ministry. During his first full term, Arthur began to transcribe the Tagalog (national language) Gospel of John into braille. The need was acute. The

World Health Organization placed the number of blind Filipinos at 700,000, and little was being done for them.

Initially, Arthur planned to produce 100 copies of the braille Gospel of John with a grant he received from World Vision. While negotiating with a commercial braille embossing company, Arthur learned that the Lutheran Braille Workers of Yucaipa, California were embossing braille literature without charge and distributing it free around the world. Arthur prepared the master copy in Manila, sent it to Yucaipa and soon received the first 500 copies of the Gospel of John in Tagalog. Additional funds for the project were supplied by the Christoffel Blindenmission of West Germany.

Today, Arthur has five co-workers transcribing the entire New Testament into braille in eight major languages of the Philippines. They are also putting the New Testament onto cassette tape for the sightless who cannot read braille, and in large print editions for those who still have limited vision.

Arthur's bright mind has conceived other projects as well. Two of his assistants are constantly out in the field, noting the number and location of sightless Filipinos, discovering which languages they speak and which medium— braille, cassette, large print—best meets their need for Scripture portions.

Arthur is compiling and computerizing a national registry of blind Filipinos—information which will be shared with the appropriate agencies. He is lobbying for free mailing privileges for the blind, making it possible to send books and equipment at no charge throughout the Philippines—a privilege already extended in 134 countries of the world. In addition, Arthur is seeking to interest other mission agencies in the evangelization of the blind by using the Scriptures he has transcribed.

Inez continues to use her nursing skills to minister to the physical needs of missionaries and nationals. She has learned how to operate a teletype machine. And she uses her counseling gift with skill and compassion.

An Honest Look Backward

"Now, don't misunderstand," Arthur is quick to point out. "It hasn't been all peaches and cream" (or more appropriately in the Philippines, "mangoes and coconut milk").

"Managing a guest house is a lot like living in a fish bowl, being on call night and day. Our missionaries came to Manila from time to time for rest, conferences, business matters.

"We also had to get used to the heat and heavy rains. And of course, there was the usual assortment of culture shocks—odors from the markets and open sewers, dickering over the price of everything, frequent interruptions in electricity, the casual Filipino attitude toward time. For me personally, being blind made it difficult to get around by myself. And the erratic phone system made it difficult to get my job done."

But life overseas is not without its rewards. Many people assume the children of missionaries are deprived of a normal upbringing by having to grow up on the mission field.

"Not necessarily so," Arthur responds. "Missionary kids—M.K.s—have the advantage of traveling, seeing other cultures, gaining a more objective view of their own culture and observing the transforming effect of newly translated Scripture."

A Final Word

Has Arthur ever had second thoughts about the decision he made changing careers at the age of 48? Any regrets about the new direction of his life?

"Absolutely no regrets or disappointments about the decision we made," he affirms. "We have known from the moment of our decision that this was right for us. We have experienced tremendous self-fulfillment and consider ourselves fortunate to be full-time ambassadors for Christ. For us, there is no higher calling, nothing we would rather do, nothing that would count for more."

For a sightless missionary, that's saying—and seeing—a lot!

3
CLOSED DOORS, OPEN WINDOWS
John and Lois Kyle

From the shores of Iwo Jima as an 18-year-old navy man, to a responsible position with a major grocery store chain, to an Atlanta seminary, to a church deep in the mountains of Kentucky, to the steamy islands of the Philippines.

Indeed, John Kyle's path has taken many interesting twists and turns. Not bad for a man whose ambition in life was to be a produce buyer. But perhaps even more significant than his *successes* are his seeming *failures*—the closed doors that could have discouraged him from ever reaching the mission field. After all, how many people do you know who have:

- been counseled against going to seminary—and still went?
- been turned down by the world's largest mission board and later returned to join that same mission?
- worked for years to achieve a key promotion in the business world—only to turn it down when it finally came?

Yet, as you'll soon discover, when God closes a door, He opens a window for those who—like John Kyle—are willing to keep their eyes fixed on Him.

———————

John was born in San Diego, California. Because his father had contracted tuberculosis, John's summers were spent in Colorado to give his father more rest. There John developed his early interest in the produce business. During the summer months he worked on a farm packing vegetables for sale in the East. Returning to school in the fall, he worked in the produce department of a large grocery store.

World War II interrupted John's annual "migration" to Colorado. He joined the navy, and after boot camp was immediately sent to Iwo Jima, where he took part in the firefight to capture that island fortress. Although 5,000 U.S. servicemen lost their lives in the battle, John's life was spared—for reasons not totally clear to him at the time.

When the war was over, John returned to the States and enrolled at Oregon State University, graduating with a degree in agriculture and business. Now he was ready to return to his first love. He went to work for Safeway Stores as a buyer and immediately began moving up the ladder in his chosen profession.

But even as John was succeeding in business, he was failing at home. At Oregon State he had met Lois; shortly after, they were married. But soon troubles developed and the marriage experienced a rapid deterioration.

Auld Lang Syne for a New Saint

John had grown up in a non-Christian home. His visits to

church were infrequent, usually on Easter Sunday. When the Kyle's marriage threatened to fall apart, Lois began to attend church by herself in a desperate search for help. There she found the answers she sought in the person of Jesus Christ.

Lois recounts that decision and the change it brought. "Our marriage was very rocky at that point. After I accepted Christ I began to pray for John. Deep down I knew John needed Christ too. But I had to wonder if it would really be possible for him to accept Christ. I was convinced our lives and marriage could be salvaged if we both were together in the Lord. I prayed much. Our pastor, Dr. Robert Munger, gave me some wise counsel at that point. He suggested in addition to prayer, the best thing I could do was to allow John to see the new Lois Kyle, now totally sold out to Jesus Christ."

Lois followed her pastor's counsel. And it began to work as John noticed the dramatic change in his marriage partner. Three months later the church sponsored a conference for young couples. John and Lois attended. And there Lois's prayers were answered as John accepted Christ on New Years Eve, at the age of 28.

"Three things happened right away," John says. "One, my life began to change dramatically. Two, Lois and I saw our marriage problems start to dissolve. Three, a Wycliffe missionary from Peru and a couple working with the Navigators began to spend time with us, deepening our commitment to God's Word and prayer. In addition, Pastor Bob Munger told me to get a world map and begin to pray for the world. I not only started growing spiritually, I also developed a growing awareness of world missions."

John began helping in a ministry to international students at the University of California at Berkeley. He was involved with men's prayer groups and Bible studies, and later worked with a Young Life group at the church. When Billy Graham came to San Francisco in 1958, John was active as a counselor during the crusade and participated in evangelistic house calls following the crusade. But the best was yet to come.

The Promotion of a Lifetime

Some time after John's conversion, Safeway offered him the promotion he had always sought. Even as a teenager working in the produce department part-time after school, he had dreamed of having the position he was now being offered. With his training, experience, and administrative abilities, John's continued advancement with the company was virtually assured.

It must have come as a surprise, therefore, when John turned down the promotion. "The reason I said no," John explains, "was so I could grow more in my Christian life. If I had accepted the promotion, I would have had to move to another city where such Christian growth would have been difficult. That decision was definitely a turning point in my life. I put Christ first before my own desire for personal success, which was very strong at that point in my life.

"I determined that God was starting to redirect my life. I resigned from Safeway to be free to let the Lord give me that direction. I needed to break my former ties with the business world that I dearly loved, in order to be totally available to God. For the next few years I worked at several different jobs in order to have time to invest in lay ministries through my local church. All the while I was listening intently to hear what God had to say about the future course of my life."

Finding a Man to Stand in the Gap

Through his own personal Bible study, reinforced by contacts with missionaries, John learned about the Great Commission—the call to take the gospel to every creature. One Sunday evening, after a medical doctor had preached from Ezekiel 22:30, John and Lois went forward to commit themselves publicly to "stand in the gap" for God.

But they didn't stop with that initial commitment. While remaining active in their lay ministries, John and Lois met weekly with another couple to pray together about their involvement in full-time ministry. They also sought the counsel of their pastor and Christian friends. The counsel they received did not always point in the same direction!

One minister counseled John to become a lay pastor, doing pastoral work for a local church. Another counseled him that he should go to seminary—an idea that sounded good to John initially, until he remembered that he was a 32-year-old married man with a wife and four children to support. Financially, seminary seemed out of the question.

In the midst of this conflicting counsel, John made his initial decision and presented himself to his presbytery as a seminary candidate. The conclusion of the presbytery was not particularly heartening, as John recalls. "The psychological tests did not confirm seminary as the best route for me. They showed that—at 32—I was too old to be going to seminary."

Untie That Sailboat

John continued to seek counsel. "I talked to one of our elders and shared with him my frustration. I felt that possibly God was calling me to become a pastor, that the denomination required seminary in order to do that, but that the leaders had counseled me against going to seminary because of my age and large family."

A couplet from Goethe, while not Scripture, contains some sage advice:

> *What you can do, or dream you can, begin it.*
> *Boldness has genius, power and magic in it.*[1]

The elder gave John some equally wise counsel: "A sailboat will not sail unless it is cast away from the dock." John adds, "He encouraged me to get moving and then allow God to open or close doors along the way." Untying the twin anchors of house and job, John set sail for Atlanta, Georgia to enroll in Columbia Seminary.

Lois was now faced with a surprise—and a struggle. "I was very pleased that John wanted to go to seminary. We both shared a growing burden for the lost. And we both had been involved in evangelism with the Internationa l Students Organization and other groups. But I was absolutely amazed that my husband— John Kyle—the man who would stop and humbly bow whenever he passed a Safeway store, was now seriously preparing to go into full-time Christian service. That was truly a surprise."

Lois in her twin roles as wife and mother had yet another struggle to conquer. "Although John and I had prayed about his new career, I still wrestled with the thought of having to leave our dream house that we had recently purchased. I didn't relish the idea of having to pack up our brood of six and move to a new area—from the West Coast to the Deep South. It wasn't my idea of fun, and to be honest I wasn't looking forward to it."

My administrative gifts and training in the business world have been fully used. My sales experience has been utilized. I truly feel that God can—and will—use mature people and their training and gifts in Christian service. In fact, I have tried to encourage many others to leave their secular occupations and enter full-time Christian service."

—John Kyle

Dandelions and Beans

John's three years in seminary were part of the necessary stepping stones for future ministry. John and Lois learned dependence upon the Lord as never before in their married life. "While in seminary, things were very tight financially. We discovered at one point that eating dandelion greens, which I would dig up from our lawn, mixed with beans, would get us by. I asked my neighbor if he minded my digging up his dandelions. He thought I was just being a good neighbor. Little did he know I was doing it in order to have something to put on the table to eat."

It was a lean and trim John Kyle who graduated from seminary three years later!

Closed Doors and Open Hearts

While in seminary John developed a burden for the Bible-less tribes of the world—the 300-million people whose languages have never been reduced to writing and thus had nothing of God's Word in their native tongue. After graduation, he applied to Wycliffe Bible Translators and headed for Wycliffe's Summer Institute of Linguistics training program at the University of Oklahoma. In three days it became obvious that John's gifts were not in the area of linguistics. Wycliffe agreed.

The door to Wycliffe closed, and another door opened—this one for home mission work in the mountainous coal mining camps of Hazard, Kentucky. Moving from the wide open spaces and academic atmosphere of Berkeley, California to the country atmosphere of a mining community in Kentucky was a giant step, and the adjustments were not easy.

When missionaries go to a foreign country, they are often greeted rather cooly at first by their native hosts.

John experienced that same kind of initial rejection—the Kentucky mountain people called him a "California city slicker." With patience and perseverance, John and Lois began to see fruit in their ministry among the mountain people, with whom they lived and worked for three years.

And as John preached God's Word to the hungry hearts of Kentucky coal miners, God began to stir his heart anew for the Bibleless tribes of the world.

Same Door, Different Hinges

The desire to take God's Word to the "uttermost parts of the earth" (Ps. 2:8, *KJV*) continued to grow, until finally John and Lois reapplied to Wycliffe. This time they found the door—which had previously been closed—swung open on different hinges and in a different direction.

Lois adds: "When we began to talk together about reapplying to Wycliffe, we both felt definitely we should do it. But Wycliffe insisted that I have a call too, and not simply accompany my husband in the sense of 'where John leads, I'll follow.'

"One day I was reading the Scriptures seeking God's direction and confirmation. This particular day God gave me three verses of assurance that I was going over the waters to many islands to serve the saints."

When it became apparent the Kyles were to leave the U.S.A. and cross the Pacific to the Philippines—a country made up of over 7,000 islands—to serve as support personnel with Wycliffe Bible Translators, the peace of God came to Lois like a flood. "Whenever things got a little tough, I would just look back on those verses of assurance God gave me while still in Kentucky, and claim them all over again."

And so it was in 1964 that John—at age 38—

accompanied by his wife Lois and four children, joined the Wycliffe family, not to work as Bible translators, but to undergird the work of Bible translation by assisting in the "business" side of the mission.

As with most "faith missions," Wycliffe missionaries are responsible to raise their own financial support. This led to some memorable moments for the Kyle family. John recalls one example of God's provision:

"A pastor in Virginia kept telling me he wanted our family to come to his church to present the work we planned to do with Wycliffe. Finally, we set out from Oregon to Virginia—2,500 miles away, and before long our car had broken down and couldn't be repaired.

"Eventually we arrived in Virginia. Sunday morning before the church service, the pastor interviewed me on his radio program. He asked how much monthly support our family still lacked. Cautiously, I said it was nearly all provided for. But he pressed me for a figure, and I finally admitted that we still needed $300 a month, an enormous sum in 1964. In addition, we needed $1,600 for our boat tickets.

"The pastor asked me, 'How are you going to raise all that money in just two months?'

"'My Father's got a lot of wealth.'

"'Whew, I was worried there for a minute. What does your father do?'

"'He owns the cattle on a thousand hills.'"

"'That's our heavenly Father too,' the pastor told his radio audience.

"The morning after the service, the missions committee met and gave us a check for $1,600, the last funds in their account, and promised us $300 monthly support, which they faithfully sent during all our years of overseas service."

For six years the Kyles worked with Wycliffe in the Philippines. John served in numerous capacities. He set up a buying department to keep the missionaries in the remote areas of the Philippines supplied with food and other essentials, a job ideally suited for a man with John's background in produce and procurement. He also served as the administrative officer for Wycliffe in Manila, as well as director of public relations, working directly with the Filipino government.

Hold on Tight

While serving in the Philippines, John had an interesting experience with a visiting pastor. "I could not afford a car, so I rode a motor scooter all around Manila. That can be quite dangerous and hair-raising at times with the traffic going in all directions, open manholes, sudden rainstorms—the works.

"A pastor from the United States came to visit, and I took him for a ride on the scooter with me. There was no ulterior motive on my part. I was just getting him around Manila.

"But immediately upon returning home, he urged his congregation to send us money for a car. He also called another friend, and together their churches raised enough money for the car. The moral of that story is, it pays for pastors visiting the mission field to experience what their missionaries are doing—and riding!"

In 1972, Wycliffe asked John to return to the United States and become a nationwide recruiter of more missionaries to complete the task of Bible translation. A year later, the newly organized Presbyterian Church in America (PCA) requested John to help them. PCA leaders were well aware of John's administrative talents. They asked him to come and set up their new mission endeavor, appropriately titled "Mission to the World." Working for three years in an on-loan capacity from Wycliffe, John provided guidance and policy-shaping direction for Mission to the World, which continues to play an increasingly significant role in missions today.

Wycliffe next asked John to launch a new International Relations Division. Out of his work came the Townsend Institute of International Relations in Washington, D.C. to train Christian diplomats.

One after another, doors continued to open for this multi-talented servant of God, culminating in his present appointment as U.S. Missions Director for InterVarsity Christian Fellowship (IVCF). John's responsibilities now include guiding the missions program for IVCF on 900 American campuses, directing the triennial Urbana Conventions, at which 17,000 college students congregate for a concentrated time of missions input and challenge: overseas training camps, student training in missions, missions counseling and much more. A tall assignment, to be sure, but John's Spirit-guided abilities seem equal to the task.

After serving for several years with distinction at InterVarsity, John was asked to return to the leadership of Mission To The World, the mission arm of the Presbyterian Church in America, where he currently works.

And with all that, John has not neglected his first and most important mission field: his family. All four of the Kyle children are serving the Lord today as missionaries somewhere in the world.

A Final Word

"I found it difficult while in seminary," John reflects, "to understand why it was necessary to take certain courses in preparation for the pastorate. My time of ministry in Kentucky was difficult at times, but we stuck with it. My first term in the Philippines was difficult, but that's not unusual for a first-term missionary. I believe the decisions we made as a family have been honored by the Lord, and we have no regrets about anything we have done.

"My administrative gifts and training in the business world have been fully used. My sales experience has been utilized. I truly feel that God can—and will—use mature people and their training and gifts in Christian service. In fact, I have tried to encourage many others to leave their secular occupations and enter full-time Christian service.

"I look back with amusement over one experience I had while I was selling copying machines before entering seminary. There was a prize for the man and his wife who sold the most machines in a single month: a trip to Hawaii. I won the Western States Division prize in June 1958. But I did not accept the prize because we planned to go to seminary in August.

"We were disappointed at the time not to be able to take that trip, little realizing that as we were faithful God would send us not only to Hawaii but around the world several times in our duties with Wycliffe, PCA and IVCF.

"You can have Hawaii," John remarks sincerely. "I'll take the world!"

Note

1. Public domain.

4

DEALING FOR THE LORD

Howard and Thelma Jones

A poster hangs over Howard Jones's desk entitled "A
Golfer's Prayer":

> May the good Lord grant,
> Before my golfing days are done,
> That I might just once
> Score a hole-in-one.[1]

It's natural for Howard to harbor such a dream, for he
is truly a "natural" in many ways. Swinging a golf club,
striking up a conversation with a total stranger, closing a
sale, sharing a word of testimony about his Savior—they
all come with disarming ease.

But there was a time in Howard's life when other
things came "naturally" too: compulsive gambling, heavy
drinking, chain-smoking and the kind of convenient "honesty" which gives used car dealers a bad name!

Today you'll find Howard, not in the showroom of an
automobile dealership, but on the staff of an Orlando, Florida church where he is finding a natural outlet for his talents and gifts in a muscular ministry to men. That's a long

way from "tee to green," as they say, so let's back up and walk the fairway with this choice servant of the Lord.

———————————

Traditionally, when a golfer "shoots his age" (finishes 18 holes using no more strokes than he has years of age) it is considered the sign of a superior athlete. If so, what must that say about Howard Jones, who recently at age 69 *shot a 66 on a par 70 course* and is today the defending seniors champion for the state of North Carolina!

Howard was seemingly born with a natural, grooved swing. Caddying gave him an excuse to prowl his favorite haunt—the local golf course. Tournament play soon followed, and before long he was good enough to turn pro. Many encouraged him to do precisely that.

In thinking back to those days, Howard reminisces: "I was good, no doubt about it, and I had a lot of people who wanted to meet me and play golf with me. I enjoyed meeting all those important people, the country club atmosphere, the money."

Howard took a job at General Motors. Though he was well-paid and on his way up the corporate ladder, he always knew where he could turn if he needed some extra money—to another of his "natural" talents: gambling. Many of Howard's friends were concerned. They felt his drinking and gambling were destroying his family and marriage. Though he wouldn't admit it, powerful addictions were taking control of his life.

A Little Child Shall Lead Them

Howard loved his family. It had taken seven years of courting before Thelma had consented to become his wife.

Come to think of it, Thelma's father had taken some convincing, too! When Thelma announced that she wanted to marry Howard, he responded, "Are you going to marry *that* thing?"

Recalling his own religious upbringing, Howard made sure the family went to church on Sunday. "I might have a hangover and headache from drinking the night before," he recalls, "but I would still go to church. In my heart I knew it was important and the right place to be."

One particular Sunday, a communion service was scheduled, a high and holy celebration in Howard's estimation. But he knew things weren't right between himself and God. "I just couldn't bring myself to take communion. In our church you went to the altar rail and knelt to receive the elements. Because I wouldn't go, Thelma didn't go either. As we were sitting there, my son began to cry."

"What's wrong, Bobby?" Howard asked.

Bobby sobbed, "Why can't I go down front for communion like all of my friends are doing?"

His son's words stabbed through Howard's heart like a knife. After the service, he told Thelma and Bobby that he didn't know when he would be going to another communion service, but when he did, he would be ready for it.

Dealing with God Before the Dawn

Several weeks passed. One evening Howard was out enjoying his favorite pastime—poker. He returned home late and lay down to get some sleep. But sleep wouldn't come. The normally comfortable bed was seemingly hard as pavement. So Howard gave up the notion of *sleeping*, and tried some *soul-searching* instead.

"I thought of my godly mother who had set such a Christian example for me. I thought of my wife who had put up with me so patiently, so lovingly. I thought of the stabbing feeling in my heart that Sunday morning at the communion service. It all came washing over me like a flood. And suddenly I realized that I had a choice to make that night."

A Chat with "Ole Buddy"

Howard knelt down beside his bed, a posture and place where he had seen his mother on many occasions. To some, the prayer that followed might have sounded sacrilegious, but for Howard it was just the honest, heartfelt way of talking to God.

"I simply prayed, 'Ole Buddy!'—and that made me sense how close He really was. 'Ole Buddy, you've been bugging me for several years, and I'm tired of it. I don't want to run any more. From now on, everything I am or ever will be, everything I have—my family, my job, my house—it's all yours.'

"When I got up off my knees, I had such a sense of peace. I laid down on that rock-hard bed and was asleep before my head hit the pillow. I discovered there wasn't a thing wrong with that bed after all. I slept like a baby the rest of the night."

Howard was 32 years old when he made his commitment to Jesus Christ, joining the slender ranks of those Christians—only 4 percent according to one survey—who first met the Savior after the age of 30.

New Light for a New Life

Howard describes his first morning as a new Christian: "As I awakened, I looked at the bedroom where I had been sleeping for several years, and it was the most beautiful room I had ever seen. I looked over at my wife, and she was even more beautiful than before. I went into my children's bedrooms, and it was the same there. Everything was so clean and beautiful!

"And just as surely as I'm talking to you now, I knew the Lord was saying, 'Howard, that's what I have done with your life. I cleaned it up just like that.'"

The Bible promises that "if any man is in Christ, he is a new creature; the old things passed away; behold, new things have come" (2 Cor. 5:17, *NASB*). And so it was in Howard's life.

His appetite for alcohol was gone. He simply had no need for it any more. The desire to gamble, once an even stronger compulsion than the desire to drink, proved more difficult. Although Howard never touched a playing card after his conversion, 20 years would pass before he felt safe around a deck of cards. It took two years to kick the three-pack-a-day cigarette habit.

Howard's former circle of friends could scarcely help noticing the change. "I had one friend," Howard recalls, "who used to give me a case of whiskey every month. A whole case, mind you. **Every month!** I prayed for him for 10 years and he finally became a Christian too."

Counting the Cost

Howard was still working at General Motors, but now he found that *selling cars* and *serving God* can sometimes create a "conflict of interests"—at least in the eyes of the management!

His boss called him in and warned him that his new interest in religion could ruin his effectiveness with the customers. Howard patiently explained that he had found what made life worth living, and that he had every intention of continuing in this new way. He graciously informed his boss that if he lost his job because of his new life in Christ, it would be worth it.

It wasn't long before Howard's boss called him into his office again—this time not to fire him, but to promote him! "I had risen in three years to the position it had taken my boss 15 years to achieve. But I guess when the Lord changed me, one of the changes was to make me an even better worker."

Dealing for the Lord

Like many in the automotive industry, Howard dreamed of owning his own dealership, preferably in a small town where he could work closely with the community. And now that opportunity came in an unlikely place: London, Kentucky. There Howard became active in church and civic affairs, always eager to share a word about the One who had made such a dramatic change in his life.

Before long, Howard's office began to double as a chapel and prayer room as hurting individuals sought his counsel. "At one time I was working with eight alcoholics. They would come to me, and I would pray for them and try to help them."

Among them was the local golf pro. He and Howard had often played together. "It was obvious alcohol was taking over and destroying his life, just as it had mine." One night in the clubhouse parking lot, they talked for over three hours. The golf pro said that for years he had been observing Howard on the golf course, on the job, in the home, and he saw a consistency that attracted him to whatever made Howard tick.

There among the tools of his trade, like Peter among the fishnets or Matthew at the tax collector's booth, the

*A*s I look back and see the direction my life has taken, I have no regrets. Well, on second thought, there are a few. I regret at times that I did not obey Him sooner. I regret that I didn't get saved earlier in life. As I think back over my first 30 years or so, I regret that I wasn't doing something for the Lord then. But the Lord took my natural abilities, sanctified them and put them to use for His purposes.

—Howard Jones

golf pro gave his life to Jesus Christ. He later went on to seminary, graduating at age 40, and today is in the ministry.

Often when Howard shared his testimony, he would hear this question: "How can you be in the automobile business and still be a Christian?"

His answer was disarmingly honest: "How can you be in *your* line of work and still be a Christian? Business is business, so long as it is reputable. My business is a good way for me to witness to people. I can give them honest deals and still make a living."

A Growing Love for Laymen

During his years in London, Howard traveled extensively speaking to laymen about the opportunities for involvement in their local church. Next came part-time work with the Philpot Evangelistic Association, where he helped organize finance committees for their evangelistic crusades.

"Each time before I left my office, I would pray: 'Now Lord, I'm leaving to do some work for you and I'm trusting you to take good care of my business while I'm gone.' And frequently, He would bring in more business while I was away than when I was there!"

From time to time Howard felt the urge to put his business up for sale and begin to work full-time with the crusade ministry. "I was ready to sell out and go," he recalls. "I can't explain it or tell you exactly how it happened, but the Lord made it clear He was not leading in that direction."

For several years Howard worked part-time in the Development Department of Asbury Theological Seminary. Again he wondered, "Is this where the Lord wants me to invest the rest of my life?" And again, the answer from the Lord came back: No.

Then at age 58, Howard suffered a massive heart attack. For a while his life hung in the balance. The lengthy recuperation process gave him many months to think, pray and meditate on the future direction of his life.

"What do you want me to do, Lord? And when? And where?" At first, God's answers weren't too clear—or encouraging. "Rather than give me a timetable for my future, He seemed to be saying, 'Howard, just trust me, and I'll show you a step at a time.'"

Three years later, having fully recovered from his heart attack, Howard Jones made a heartfelt commitment: "Lord, I'm getting out of the automobile business. Whatever it is you want me to do, I'm willing to do it." Howard was 61.

Not My Will, But Thine

A pastor friend of Howard's approached him about accepting a position at his church in Louisville. Howard would be in charge of ministering to the men of the church, helping them in their roles as Christian businessmen, husbands and fathers. The challenge was exactly what Howard was seeking.

"This was the ideal situation for me. I was confident I had at last found God's perfect place of service. I would be involved with laymen, something I had always enjoyed. Louisville was home. Both of my children lived there. I would be near my grandchildren. Everything seemed to say the position was tailor-made for me. There was just one problem: the Lord wasn't in it."

A lengthy "debate" followed between Howard and his heavenly Father. "I talked to the Lord as earnestly as I dared, and asked Him if He really understood the situation as well as I did. It was quite obvious to me that this was exactly where I ought to be, doing what I enjoyed doing best. But the Lord wouldn't let me make that commitment. It's difficult to explain in theological terms. All I can say is, the Lord wouldn't allow me to have any peace when I thought about going there."

Closed Doors, Open Doors

Howard and Thelma took a much-needed vacation to Florida. While there, Howard received a call from another pastor friend in Orlando. A search committee from his church was interviewing candidates for a newly added staff position, and Howard was invited to apply. The job? *Heading up a ministry to laymen!*

Howard confesses with a smile, "I told him I would be glad to come and talk with them, but my real motive was having an excuse to play golf with the pastor."

After the committee had interviewed him, they extended an immediate invitation to join the staff. Howard told them he wasn't even sure he *wanted* the job. But he promised to pray about it and let them know.

Returning to Kentucky, Howard wrestled in prayer once again to seek the Lord's mind and find His clear direction. "I can't explain how the Lord talked to me. And when I say talk, I don't mean in any audible voice. He didn't come up to me, pull my ear, and say 'Get going, buddy!' But as Thelma and I talked and prayed together, there came a deep peace of mind for both of us that this was what we should do."

And that was how, at *age 62*, Howard joined the staff of the Pine Castle United Methodist Church in Orlando, Florida. Did he ever have second thoughts about deciding *not* to take the church position in Louisville? "God's confirmation was so precious," he responds with a chuckle. "Three months after we moved to Orlando, the pastor in Louisville, the one I would have worked with, moved to another church. If I had gone there directed by my own will instead of God's, I would have barely gotten started before the pastor left. And who knows what plans the new pastor would have brought with him! So I see it as God's sovereign hand of direction."

What is Howard doing today? For several years he headed up an exciting ministry in Orlando which challenges men to "come alive" to the claims of Jesus Christ in their personal, family and business lives. Under his leadership, Howard had seen scores of men assume positions of spiritual leadership in their homes and communities, and become active witnesses for Jesus Christ. "I've never enjoyed anything as much as I enjoyed this work!"

God's Word for a Fearful Heart

One day during a routine physical examination, Howard learned he had an irregular heartbeat. He didn't think too much about it, took the medicine his doctor prescribed and went on his way.

Later that same week Howard read an article in *Decision* magazine. "I don't even remember what the article was about or who wrote it. And really, only one line from the article stuck in my mind. But it was something special. I actually called out to Thelma and said, 'Honey, listen to this.'"

The line was a verse from the Psalms: "When I am afraid, I trust in thee." There was no reference given for the verse. The next morning, Howard went hunting to discover where it was found.

"I started with the first Psalm and read straight through to the thirty-fifth. No luck. So I started at the back, in Psalm 150, and read backwards to Psalm 119. Still nothing. The next morning I started at Psalm 36 and headed 'East' again. Finally in Psalm 56, verse three, I found it! I read and reread that Psalm. I kept asking myself what I was afraid of. What was wrong? I didn't know. As I continued to read, I prayed, 'Lord, I don't know exactly what you're trying to say to me. But whatever it is, I am going to trust you in it.'"

Three weeks later, Howard found his answer. A second exam and further tests revealed that he had three blockages in coronary arteries—one 85 percent, one 90 percent and one 100 percent. Open heart surgery was urgently needed. "If the doctor had told me three weeks earlier, I don't know how I would have responded. But the Lord knew and had prepared me. I had tremendous peace and confidence in His care because I was trusting in Him completely."

Since the surgery, Howard has been more active than ever. After leading the Laymen's ministry in Orlando for eight years, Howard recently retired (for the second time) and is now making his home in Louisville, KY. Of course, saying Howard has "retired" doesn't do the word justice. He still maintains an active involvement in the lives of men. It couldn't be otherwise. Not with Howard Jones.

A Final Word

I asked Howard if there was anything he wished had turned out differently about the Lord's dealings in his life.

"No, as I look back and see the direction my life has taken, I have no regrets. Well, on second thought, there are a few. I regret at times that I did not obey Him sooner.

I regret that I didn't get saved earlier in life. As I think back over my first 30 years or so, I regret that I wasn't doing something for the Lord *then*. But the Lord took my natural abilities, sanctified them and put them to use for His purposes.

"I'm 69 now, and enjoying every minute of my work as a layman for Him. I guess my biggest regret would be that there aren't more people enjoying the same kind of fulfillment I've discovered."

Coming from an old golfer like Howard, I guess you could say that's par for the course.

Note

1. Source unknown.

5
THE SPICE OF LIFE
Charlie and Phylis Spicer

Charlie Spicer's prayer that morning in Shanghai was short and to the point: "Lord, lead me to someone today who speaks English well enough so I can share the gospel with him. Someone you have prepared in this large and lost city."

"Ping-Pong diplomacy" had reopened the doors of China to tourists, and Charlie intended to be one of the first! But how could he share the good news when the government forbade any lengthy conversations between residents and foreign visitors?

And what was a former insurance salesman doing in China in the first place? He was certainly not there to promote whole life policies—or was he?

When you first meet Charlie Spicer, you see eyes that dance with merriment, a cheery smile held together by a mustache and a warm expression. Much of this is Charlie's natural endowment. Some of it was developed in the insurance business. All of it has been refined by the Holy Spirit through three decades of walking with the Lord.

But ironically for a man of such warmth and good humor, it took a broken heart, a praying pastor, a firsthand look at the mission field and an empty office to turn Charlie around and point him in the direction of world missions.

Young Charlie received Christ as his Savior in a little country Methodist church in Maryland when he was eight years old. But like many new Christians, it would be decades before Charlie cultivated a grown-up relationship with his heavenly Father.

After a tour of duty with the army and studies at Johns Hopkins University, Charlie married his college sweetheart Phylis. His ambition in life: to own a successful insurance business.

Phylis grew up in the typical religious home. "My idea of religion was good works. I was living with the hope that at the end of my life, when all my deeds and misdeeds would be put on the scale, my right deeds would outweigh the wrong things I had done and so tip the scales favorably with God."

But an old-fashioned tent meeting would change all that. A local church had pitched a big tent and was holding meetings every night for two weeks.

One night the preacher brought a very simple salvation message—a message Phylis had never heard before. At the close, she raised her hand for prayer. Later in the prayer tent, the pastor's wife explained how she could know Christ personally. That night, Phylis was the only one who responded to the invitation. In fact, she was the only one who responded during the entire two weeks. "In most respects," Phylis reflects, "I guess the meetings weren't very successful." But she would be eternally grateful for that local church's vision.

While attending a Methodist church in Hampsted, Maryland, Charles and Phylis discovered another new love: missions. Don McIntosh, their pastor, had a burning heart for world evangelization. Every year the church would hold a week-long world missions conference. The pastor's wife Evelyn was a remarkably talented lady who had more ideas about missions involvement than she had hands and feet to implement. Phylis volunteered to help.

One project was a 27-foot mural about India to be used in the missions conference. Another was entertaining a missionary family in the Spicers' lovely home. "My first reaction to that one was, 'No, thank you. I'm interested in missions, but not that interested.'" But with some gentle encouragement she finally, if somewhat reluctantly, gave in.

"We just had a ball with those missionaries," Phylis recalls. "They really weren't up on any pedestal. They weren't supersaints or superweird. They were just like us. In between our fun times, I slowly began to realize my views about missions were changing. My perspective was enlarging. I really began to get a vision for reaching the whole world with the gospel."

In addition to providing hospitality and serving as "helping hands," the Spicers began a financial commitment to missions. They were challenged by the concept of a "faith promise" offering—committing a sum of money to the missions endeavor of the church beyond any visible source of funds.

"We prayed separately about what amount to commit for the year. When Charlie and I discussed it later, we found we had decided on exactly the same amount. At first it staggered us. But we agreed in faith to do it. The amount was equal to one month's salary—and God enabled us to meet every penny of it. So the next year we doubled the amount. And the year following we tripled it. Every year, God was faithful."

"Then after a few years we both felt that God was saying to us, 'Now I know I can trust you with your money. But can I trust you with your life? Are you willing to commit your whole lives to me for what I want you to do?'"

An Unusual Investment Portfolio

As chairman of the missions committee, Charlie decided he needed to make a personal visit to the mission field "to check up on our mission investments." For five weeks in 1964, Charlie traveled throughout Central and South America. The sights and sounds deeply moved him.

"In Mexico City, I saw people crawling on their knees for long distances, becoming weak in the process. Their knees were worn raw from the rough stone streets. I was told they were suffering this pain hoping to atone for their sins. But as I looked into their faces, all I saw was hopelessness and despair. It was the first time I had ever really come face-to-face with heathen darkness.

"I would watch as they rubbed their hand over an image and then took that hand and rubbed it over their baby or small child hoping to give their child some religious merit. As I watched them leave, I observed that they still had that same lost, hopeless expression. I knew I had the answer they needed to hear, but I couldn't get it out because I didn't speak Spanish."

The experience broke Charlie's heart. For the first time in his adult life he shed tears for people who were lost without Christ. "I needed to have that experience," Charlie recalls. "I needed my heart broken for the needs of people."

Later on that same trip, he spent 11 days in Colombia

with Harold Brabon of OMS International (formerly Oriental Missionary Society). The turbulent period known as *La Violencia* was in full swing, and Charlie experienced persecution firsthand.

He was harassed; nails were driven into his car tires; he was pelted with rocks; he was run out of town. But nothing could keep him from sharing his faith. "The most thrilling part of the trip for me as a layman was that every time I gave my testimony, someone got saved." This would begin a pattern in Charlie's life, combining a ringing testimony with a heart for people.

Charlie returned from his life-changing experience, eager to find another group of people to take with him on yet another trip to the mission field. But reality quickly set in, for surprisingly few shared his enthusiasm. Finally, after months of frustration, Charlie asked his pastor for a chance to present his burden one evening during the church's missions conference. "If no one is interested," he reasoned, "I'll forget about the whole thing."

After the service, a couple in their 80s came up to speak with Charlie. "If there is still room on that trip, my wife and I would like to go." They were vital and alert, but obviously feeble and frail. Charlie looked at them and prayed silently, "Lord, this can't be your confirmation, can it?" But there they stood. And as Charlie would later explain, "When you are desperate, you'll take anyone as long as they are breathing!" In all, 21 people accompanied him on the trip, including four pastors and six young people—four of whom would later go on into full-time Christian service.

Sitting in the airport in Bogota, Colombia, Charlie struck up a conversation with Margaret Brabon of OMS International, who challenged Charlie to consider working with OMS's "Men for Missions" (MFM) group which seeks to involve laymen and women in mission work projects both at home and abroad. "For the first time in my life," Charlie recalls, "I was speechless. I couldn't talk, which for me was really something. I was so filled with emotion that the tears just rolled. I couldn't even utter the word good-bye as I was leaving."

Loosening the Tent Pegs

Taking the safe, noncommittal route, Charlie promised Margaret he would certainly pray about the opportunity. A few months later another missionary friend called to talk about the same position. During the annual missions conference that year, two missionary couples stayed with the Spicers. Together, they gently and prayerfully talked about the specific need for leadership in Men for Missions. "During the week as we talked and learned more about missions, we began to feel God loosening the dirt around our roots. We didn't know the 'where' or 'what' at that point, but we could sense that our tent stakes were starting to move."

And a Little Child Shall Lead Them

The week of the missions conference was so filled with meetings, Charlie and Phylis hardly had time to talk. Wednesday evening their 13-year-old daughter rode home with a friend, giving her parents their first moments alone together. As they talked about what God seemed to be saying about missions and their future, the conversation turned to the idea of a fleece—not to *show* them what to do, but to *confirm* in their hearts what they were sensing as God's direction for their lives.

"In my case," Charlie reflects, "I needed God to do

We didn't know where we were headed or for what; but we had counted the cost and said we were ready to go."

—Charlie and Phylis Spicer

something pretty obvious and unmistakable." As they talked further, Phylis had an idea. "Charlie, you and I have been talking about becoming missionaries. But what about our daughter? I wonder if God has been speaking to her." They determined the fleece would be their daughter's response.

Ten minutes later they arrived home. As they removed their coats in the downstairs hallway, their daughter came down the stairs with tears rolling down her cheeks. "I've been praying in my bedroom about becoming a missionary, and I think God wants me to be one."

Truly a little child shall lead them. Today that 13-year-old is a lovely wife and mother, serving the Lord in Indonesia with OMS International.

Counting the Cost

Two weeks later in God's perfect timing, the Spicers heard yet another missionary speaker. He began his talk by telling about a couple in business who sold everything to become missionaries to Africa. He then spoke on counting the cost of following Christ.

That night and all the next day, Charlie and Phylis evaluated their own lives to see if they were willing to count the cost of serving the Lord. That cost included a highly successful insurance business. Charlie was a Chartered Life Underwriter (CLU) and regularly achieved the National Quality Award. His father, who was also in the insurance business, regularly sold about two-thirds of the policies to the dental school graduates from the University of Maryland. Charlie was in line to get all that business as soon as his father retired.

That evening at church when the invitation was given, the Spicers went forward hand-in-hand to offer their lives for missionary service. "At that point we didn't know where we were headed or for what; but we had counted the cost and said we were ready to go."

And how did Phylis feel about all of this? "I had read over the list of God's promises that Charlie had written down. I agreed with every one of them. But while I knew in my head they were all true, and God was who He said He was, still I had a little struggle. I was security conscious. I had a nice, comfortable 'nest' built around me. Charlie was earning good money. So when the decision process became serious and it looked like we would be joining a mission group, my first thought was, Would we be able to make it on a missionary's salary?"

Filling a Vacant Office

An important link in the chain was added a few months later. Charlie and Phylis had gone to the dedication of the new OMS office in Greenwood, Indiana. On Friday, Dale McClain, a missionary friend, gave Charlie a "sneak preview" of the office. As they walked around the halls, there was one office and one secretary's desk that were vacant, that of the national director for Men for Missions. The significance didn't escape Charlie. "It became obvious there was a need we could fill."

Later that day Charlie spoke with a missionary named Cliff who was not connected with OMS and did not know Charlie at all. During the hour they were together, Charlie shared all that had happened in the previous months. At the end, Cliff remarked, "Your experience is similar to the one I went through several years ago in making my decision. Let me give you a verse that was helpful to me. 'And now Lord, for what do I wait? My hope is in Thee' (Ps. 39:7, *NASB*)."

Returning home, Charlie and Phylis reviewed all that had happened over the past months: the conversations with various people, the fleece, their daughter's response, their counting the cost, the empty office and desk. Charlie had filled many legal pads with promises from God's Word about how to deal with change and its resulting anxiety. "It was as if God were saying, 'I've showed you an empty office and desk. I've convinced you that I'm calling you. What are you waiting for?'"

The Spicers sent a letter to OMS: "We believe we are the ones God is speaking to about helping you."

Confirmation came only days later from God's Word. "The preparations of the heart in man, and the answer of the tongue, is from the Lord" (Prov. 16:1, *KJV*). As Charlie reflected on that verse, his thought processes went something like this: "'The answer of the tongue'; we had given that the week before. What about the 'preparation of the heart'? At that point I began reviewing my whole life in the light of God's plan for it. I began to see how every experience God had permitted me to have was part of the 'preparation of the heart' that I needed before I could answer, 'Here am I, Lord' [see Acts 9:10]."

Confirmation also came from Charlie's parents. Charlie had lunch with his father to tell him of his decision. His father had only one question: "Are you sure?"

Charlie responded without a moment's hesitation, "I really know that God is in this whole thing. I can't disobey the Lord. I am sure." Charlie's parents became two of his strongest supporters. "President and vice president of my fan club, you might say."

Fine-Tuning a New Life-style

In talking about their new life as missionaries, Charlie and

Phylis honestly share one of their biggest adjustments. "It was difficult moving from an ultra-independent life-style, to letting someone else pick up the check. It took us months to gear down to a missionary budget. We finally had to cut up all our credit cards and only spend what we had in our pockets. And once we learned how to do that, from that point on we've had few problems. We've just learned to live within our allowance.

"We have wished sometimes we had the means to help our children in special financial needs. Before, that would have been no problem. But it has given us an opportunity to trust God more and see Him fulfill His promises as He supplies their needs as well as our own."

Charlie's background uniquely prepared him for his missionary responsibilities. With OMS, Charlie served first as North American director for Men for Missions, taking many laymen overseas to see missions "up close and personal." Later, he served as treasurer, and most recently as vice president for public relations and development. In his "spare" time he also serves as special assistant to the chairman for the Lausanne Committee for World Evangelization, and as president of the Overseas Council for Theological Education and Missions.

"I still marvel," Charlie remarks, "how the Lord allowed all my prior experience in the business world, experience I now draw upon virtually every day in my mission work. As an insurance man, I helped lots of people plan their wills and estates, saving them money on their taxes and helping them keep as much as possible for themselves. Now I do almost the identical thing. I help people save on their taxes, but instead of keeping as much as possible, I now help them invest in heavenly treasures.

"As a layman, I was always frustrated because I personally couldn't give more to missions, although we had doubled our giving several times. Now, God has given me the opportunity and joy of giving guidance to other people in their giving. I am able to generate more money in this way than I might ever have been able to give in an entire lifetime."

A Final Word

And so *at age 37*, Charlie Spicer became a missionary. In thinking back over his decision, Charlie had this to say: "My only regret is that I wasn't ready sooner. I love every minute of it. I've never worked harder in my life. But I've never enjoyed doing anything as much as what I'm doing now.

"There are a couple of other verses that continually motivate me: 'He who wins souls is wise' (Prov. 11:30, *NKJV*), and 'Those who are wise shall shine like the brightness of the firmament, and those who turn many to righteousness shall shine as the stars forever and ever' (Dan. 12:3, *NKJV*)."

"You just feel like giving it all you've got, letting God use you to advance His work around the world. None of us knows how long we have, so we just keep going."

One example of how Charlie "keeps going" and of how God has used him comes from his recent tour of China. During a visit to Shanghai, he prayed specifically one morning that God would lead him to someone who was prepared to receive the gospel.

After talking to several people on the street, he noticed one man step out of a group and begin to follow him. Cyril introduced himself and after a brief conversation invited Charlie to be his guest for dinner that evening at his home.

Cyril took Charlie on a bus across town, through dark

alleys, to a second-story flat. Inside were his father, two brothers, and girlfriend, all of whom spoke English. The conversation that night centered around the gospel. The girl knew quite a bit about the Bible, although she had never read one nor had even seen one.

About eleven o'clock, Charlie felt he should return so as not to arouse too much suspicion. Before leaving, he took from his pocket a little booklet entitled *Steps to Peace with God.* "May I read this to you before I go?" he asked, and they nodded in agreement. Charlie read it out loud sentence-by-sentence, then had them read it back to Him.

When they came to the suggested prayer at the end of the booklet, Charlie stopped. He felt they should not read it because it was a prayer to be used by someone wanting to invite God into his life. He didn't want to presume upon the gracious hospitality of his host family, who might be tempted to pray simply out of courtesy for their guest. But he asked if they would like him to explain what the prayer meant. Again, they nodded enthusiastically. As he explained the prayer, Charlie asked each one if that prayer expressed the desire of his or her heart. And one by one, each affirmed that it did. That evening, five Chinese found not only an earthly friend, but a heavenly Father.

Since then, the daughter of that family has come to the United States, majored in communications and graduated with honors from a Christian college. Today she is involved in broadcasting the gospel to her native China. Cyril also came to the States and is preparing for the gospel ministry. He has translated the booklet *Steps to Peace with God* into Chinese and sent copies to all his family members. With the exception of one grandmother, every single member of the family is now a Christian! All because an insurance man determined that God had a job for him to do.

Phylis adds her honest feelings: "I'm sure there have been some times when I've had second thoughts. It's been a little tough with Charlie traveling so much. I've had to be both father and mother a lot. But I think those are normal thoughts and feelings that any wife and mother would have. Yet I can definitely say it was exactly the right decision. I wholeheartedly supported Charlie during the decision-making process, and have ever since."

It's an oft-quoted saying, but unerringly true: "Many are *willing* to go; but few are *planning* to go." Number Charlie and Phylis Spicer among those who are ready, willing and able!

Section Two

FROM THE MILITARY WORLD

6
NOTHING IS NON-SURVIVABLE WITH GOD

John and Shirley Kelley

As the helicopter plunged to the ground in a ball of flames, pilot John Kelley's first thought was heavenward: *"I'll soon be seeing Jesus."*

What had begun as a routine check flight had suddenly become a flaming, plummeting nightmare. The rotor blade had gone spinning off into space, leaving the helicopter without power and out of control. Indeed, heaven seemed just a heartbeat away.

John's second thought was equally remarkable, considering the chaos in the cockpit: "This can't really be happening to me, God. Have you forgotten that I promised you I would become a missionary just as soon as I retired from the army?"

There was no time for a reply.

When the recovery team arrived at the accident site, they needed only one word to describe the crash: Nonsurvivable. In fact, it was to become the turning point in John Kelley's life.

Growing up in a one-parent family is never easy under the best of circumstances, and for John Kelley, the circumstances were anything *but* the best.

His parents had divorced when John was only five. His father received legal custody and did his best to raise John right. But work was hard to find. Gas station attendant, mechanic, truck driver. The jobs seldom lasted more than a few weeks. John and his father moved countless times during those formative years. Before he reached the tenth grade John had attended 17 different schools.

"I really didn't have a normal home environment," John admits matter-of-factly. "From the time I was 12 I pretty much raised myself. My father was constantly on the road.

"It was pretty tough on my teachers too. Whenever they asked for a parent-teacher conference, I had to think of excuses why my father couldn't come. I was afraid they would discover what kind of home I lived in, and try to change the way my father was."

John's father was not a Christian at the time, but he recognized the value of church training. Although he didn't go to church himself, he made young John attend each Sunday. John confesses, "Many times I never actually arrived! I would leave the house at the right time, walk around town until I knew church was over, then go back home."

Join the Navy and See the World

With little interest in studying, John dropped out of school in the tenth grade and joined the navy. *Anything* seemed better than the home life he was leading. His father agreed and signed the papers allowing him to join up.

There John learned the trade of a jet engine mechanic—and the rewards of hard work and self-reliance. "I discovered in the military that if I were ever going to amount to anything, I was going to have to do it myself. I had the attitude, 'As long as I'm here, I might as well fly as high as I can go.' In my four years I received many promotions and also my high school equivalency diploma."

While stationed in Jacksonville, Florida, John met Shirley. After a two-year assignment in the Philippines, he was discharged from the navy, married Shirley, and settled in California. There in the heartland of the aerospace industry, John became a flight test technician.

You're in the Army Now

The brief years in California were enjoyable, but John's earlier experience in the service had whetted his appetite for flying. John set his sights on becoming a pilot. He joined the army flight program, earning his wings as a pilot and his shoulder bars as an officer.

With his previous background in aircraft maintenance, the army sent him for more training to become a maintenance officer. In the process he became a test pilot as well. God was beginning to weave significant threads into the fabric of John's life.

The Seat Where John Should Have Sat

The Vietnam conflict was raging, and John's skills were needed there as a helicopter pilot. Only three weeks into his tour of duty, John narrowly escaped death.

Troops were being moved to new positions, and John was assigned one of the transport helicopters. Because he was newly arrived and unfamiliar with the terrain and procedures, John was assigned the copilot's seat. Just prior to takeoff, the platoon leader called to him, "Kelley! We've changed the schedule. I want you to fly copilot in another chopper."

The command was timely indeed. The helicopter in which John was originally scheduled to fly suffered a transmission failure in flight. The blades quit turning and the helicopter crashed, killing all 11 on board. John was deeply shaken.

"It was a very emotional experience for me. We were one of the first helicopters to respond after the crash. We landed and started dragging the men out, hoping to find someone still alive. As I helped remove the copilot's body, I realized that person would have been me if I had not been reassigned.

"I did thank God for saving my life, but I didn't know why He had gone to the trouble. At that time, I thought of religion as something for weak men and little old ladies. I had never read the Bible and really knew nothing about it. But I was always ready to stand up and defend it in a debate."

The rest of John's stay in Vietnam passed without incident, and he returned to Virginia to write manuals for the maintenance and repair of turbine engines. With his knowledge and experience, the army sent him to the Aeronautical University at Daytona, Florida where he finished his college degree.

Finding a Free Gift in Florida

Shirley was a Christian when she married John, but his indifference toward the church had caused her to put church attendance on the back burner of her own life as well. Now, with a young daughter to think of, Shirley encouraged John to make church a regular family activity. John had no objections.

The first Sunday they attended, the pastor preached a message from Ephesians 2:8-9. He emphasized that salvation was by grace—a free gift and not something that could be bought or earned.

John remembers that day well. "God spoke to me through that message, but I had a problem. I knew I would never be good enough to merit my salvation. But I had also seen a lot of people who claimed to be Christians and yet acted worse than I did. I knew I could not be a hypocrite. I didn't want to pretend to be something I wasn't. So I decided the answer was honesty, rather than hypocrisy. I would just take my chances with the Lord when my time came.

"I did not go forward that morning, but I did raise my hand to indicate that I had a spiritual need. I just couldn't believe salvation was as easy as the pastor said—all I had to do was accept Christ by faith."

As John left the church that morning, the pastor stopped him. "I noticed you raised your hand this morning. Would you like me to come to your home and talk with you?"

John said he would be happy for him to come. He expected the pastor to stop by on Monday. "I was ready for him," John recalls. "I wanted to get it over with because I was afraid I wouldn't go through with it if I waited too long." But Monday came and went with no pastor. Tuesday—same thing.

By the time the pastor arrived on Wednesday, John was more than ready. "He explained to me the simple plan of salvation. I acknowledged that I was a sinner and received Jesus Christ as my Savior. That night at prayer meeting I was baptized."

Coincidence or Incidents?

The following Sunday, a chance meeting with another pilot was to introduce a very important thread into the tapestry God was weaving in John's life.

Another ex-army pilot was preparing to go as a missionary pilot with Mission Aviation Fellowship (MAF). Because of their mutual interests and experiences, John was eager to talk with him.

"Now let me get this straight," John inquired. "You're going to go overseas someplace, live in a tent and make absolutely no money. Is that right? You must be crazy!"

Little did John know that before long he would join the ranks of those "crazy," wonderful missionary pilots. But for now, his only ambition was to get out of the service, hitch on with a major corporation or airline and "start making the big bucks."

Don't Touch That Dial

The next five years slipped by quickly. Wherever and whenever John and Shirley moved—and as a military family, that was often—they became active in a local church. Slowly, gradually, spiritual growth was taking place.

One evening John returned home to find the TV playing in the den, but no one watching it. He reached over to push the off button, but a familiar sound interrupted his motion. Rotor blades. That distinctive whipping, whirling sound. John sat down to see what the program was all about. Fifteen minutes later when Shirley walked into the room, she found John intently studying the program, big tears cascading down his face.

"Shirley, you've got to see this. Sit down here. This is it. This is what God wants me to do."

The program was a special about the work of MAF, showing how aircraft are being used to assist and accelerate the progress of mission work around the world.

"Shirley," John said excitedly, "this is the same organization that army pilot was with five years ago. MAF. Remember?"

John immediately wrote MAF inquiring where his chance acquaintance from the army was now serving. They started to correspond, John and Shirley began to support him monthly, and before long the Kelleys had become area representatives for MAF in and around Columbus, Georgia where John was stationed.

John's sights were now set. After retirement from the army, he would become a pilot-mechanic with MAF. God had prepared him well for the job. "My degree program was in Aviation Maintenance Management. Part of the requirements was to get my *A* and *P* (Air Frame and Power Plant) license. It is not required for the army because the army is its own licensing agency. However, I *had* to get it as part of my degree program. Later, I discovered that MAF requires each pilot to have his *A* and *P* license. God knew all along I would need that license and was preparing me in advance for what I would need to serve Him effectively!"

John was getting important practical experience in the army as well. He was the officer in charge of 29 aircraft and more than 125 men. His job: to inspect the maintenance work done and then take each aircraft for a check ride before it could be certified for service. One such flight would soon alter his life forever.

During this time John was talking with his pastor about becoming a missionary pilot. The pastor encouraged John to pursue the direction he felt God was leading. So John wrote to MAF, expressing his desire to join their team. At this point, he had 16 years in the army.

John also wrote army headquarters in Washington about resigning his commission in the army. They responded by reminding him that he had just received another promotion and was obligated for two more years before they could consider his request.

The MAF leaders wrote their counsel: "You can't get out of the army for two years anyhow. In another two years beyond that, you would have your 20 years and could receive your retirement benefits. We recommend you finish your career in the military." Then the letter added, "You should stay in the military—*unless some unusual or specific prodding or circumstance comes from the Lord!*"

Little did the writer of that letter know how prophetic his words would become.

The Struggle Continues

Although John was excited about the ministry opportunities with MAF, he still wasn't sure. A struggle was raging between *John's* will for John's life, and *God's* will for John's life. It would come to a head at—of all places—a missions banquet.

Thanksgiving season, 1979. John and Shirley accompanied the pastor and his wife to a special banquet honoring 94 missionaries who would soon be headed to the field. Several shared their testimony during the evening, and one in particular caught John's attention. It was virtually a carbon copy of his own life situation. An air force pilot had felt the Lord calling him into full-time service, had struggled with the decision for several years, finally left the military, went to seminary and was now on his way to the mission field.

John was convicted. "I felt that God was saying He really wanted me to 'come clean' with Him. I finally faced up to the fact that I had been playing games with God. I was saying in essence, 'Lord, I'll serve you when I'm ready, and on my terms. When I finish my army career, then I'll serve you.' But I knew deep down that I wouldn't! I was excited about MAF, but I was also thinking of retiring and getting a lucrative flying job. I hadn't been able to face myself honestly until that night."

After the banquet, the pastor noticed that something was deeply troubling John.

"What's wrong, John? You seem upset."

"I am upset." John went on to explain the struggle he was experiencing. After he finished, they prayed together.

"I'll never forget what I prayed," John recalls. "It went something like this: 'God, if I'm making a vow or swearing deceitfully to you, then I ask you to take my life. I don't want to live the rest of my life with the tormenting thought that you want me to do something I'm not willing to release myself to do.'"

A Day Like No Other

John went to work the next day as usual. It would seemingly be a day like countless others. Three helicopters had been repaired. John would take them up, check them out and certify them as ready to be put back into operation. Routine stuff.

Shortly after takeoff, John sensed that something was wrong. With a screech of metal, the main rotor blade tore free and went spinning off into the air. Without power and out of control, the helicopter became a flaming ball of twisted metal as it plummeted toward the swampy Georgia landscape below. All John could do was ride it to the ground—and pray.

"Several things went racing through my mind during those brief seconds before we crashed. One, I discovered that I was not afraid to die. This business of eternal life and the assurance of salvation is for real! Two, I found myself praying, 'Lord, this can't really be happening to me. I'm yours. I'm serving you.' But I realized it was. I also knew that I wasn't going to live through the ordeal. When you loose a rotor blade it is the equivalent of loosing a wing on a plane. I knew I was going to be meeting the Lord in just a few seconds. I had a fleeting thought of my wife and daughter, that I wouldn't be seeing them that day."

Those thoughts were interrupted by the bone-crushing impact.

"We went into some trees. After the initial contact, I didn't see, hear or feel anything. When I finally opened my eyes, all I could see was twisted metal and wreckage. I could hear and smell the flames at the back of the aircraft and felt the heat moving toward me. When I realized I was still on earth and not in heaven, I was momentarily disappointed because I had been looking forward to seeing the Lord. I pinched myself. I just couldn't believe I was still alive.

"I unbuckled my seat belt and shoulder harness, and immediately fell on my head, not realizing until then that the aircraft had come to rest upside-down. I tried to stand up twice, but couldn't. I kept falling down and couldn't figure out what was wrong. Then I looked down and saw my right foot twisted 90 degrees from where it ought to be."

A fellow crew member had miraculously been thrown free of the wreckage. The cargo doors were jammed shut and could not be opened. The whole front of the helicopter had been sheared off, as if by an enormous band saw.

"I heard someone yelling at me from outside the cockpit. To this day I'm not sure who he was or how he got

I know that many times people seem to put missionaries on a pedestal, as if they were some kind of super special breed of people. But I know that God can use just plain, ordinary people as well, because that's all I am."

—John Kelley

there. He asked me how I was. I thought I was okay, and told him to get the copilot out. On impact his seat had been turned completely around and was jammed against the back section of the helicopter. He was dead."

With the help of the surviving crew member, John left the wreckage. They had only gone about 75 feet when the entire helicopter exploded in a blinding fireball.

In the write-up following the crash, the army called it a "nonsurvivable" accident. But miraculously, John had survived. God had other plans for his servant.

The leg injury was a severe one, to be sure, but John was confident that six months in a cast would fix all that. In reality, it would be more than two full years, as John was to learn so painfully. At first, it seemed the only hope for survival would involve amputation of the whole leg. One of the surgeons, a veteran of Vietnam, had worked on many cases as severe as John's. He felt it might yet be possible to save the leg and foot. After several hours of surgery, the limb was placed in a hip-length cast and the long process of healing began.

The Smell of Death

But healing did not happen. The doctors called it a "nonunion," which is medical lingo for bones that refuse to knit together properly. A full year came and went, and still the leg and foot were not healing. Worse yet, the leg was constantly draining. John recalls that difficult period. "To be honest, I smelled like a dead animal. I really don't know how my wife put up with sleeping in the same room with me.

"I tried buying those small round stick-on deodorants, and would stick them on the cast. But it didn't really help. I would get on an elevator and people would start sniffing and commenting: 'Boy, it smells like there must be some dead rats down the elevator shaft!' I would just stand there hoping they didn't discover who it was that was smelling like dead rats.

"One night I went to a big conference at our church. Usually the front rows were pretty empty. I had a stool up front and would sit on the first row with my cast propped up on the stool. But this particular night the place was packed. Every row was crammed. I came in, sat down and put my leg up on the little stool. In a few minutes—a very few minutes—I looked around and discovered I had emptied the entire front three rows."

John's spirits hit an all-time low.

Calling All Elders

One Wednesday evening, John and Shirley went to the prayer service at their church. At the conclusion, the pastor asked, as was his custom, if anyone had a special need for prayer. John recalls every detail of that pivotal evening.

"As the pastor asked that question, I fell apart. I began to sob. I got my crutches and hobbled up front. I told the pastor I knew he had already been praying for me, but I felt I needed some new strength. My big problem was coming to the place where I could accept the amputation of my leg, if that's what it took. Because it had been over a year since the accident and still the healing process had not begun, the doctors were talking amputation as the only solution. Something had to happen—I just couldn't go on any longer with things as they were."

The pastor said he would like to do something he normally did not do, but something that was definitely scriptural. "Is anyone among you sick? Let him call for the elders of the church, and let them pray over him" (Jas.

5:14, *NKJV*). The pastor requested all the elders and deacons to come down front, lay hands on John and together pray for God's perfect will to be done in his life.

"As they began praying, my mind and heart were flooded with indescribable peace. I knew then that God could use me *with* or *without* two legs."

Z Marks the Spot

Two weeks later, John went to have the cast changed, a ritual he had observed countless times. Normally when the cast was removed, the foot would simply flop over and lay flat on the table. But this time, to everyone's amazement, the foot stood up straight as it should. The doctor looked on in disbelief. Taking hold of John's foot and gently moving it from side to side, the doctor exclaimed, "Your foot is starting to heal! It isn't solid yet. It feels like Jello in there. But it is definitely starting to fuse back together. I just didn't expect it to happen this fast."

If the truth were known, the doctor probably wasn't expecting it to happen at all. The healing was the direct result of prayer, and John lost no time sharing that fact with the doctor.

For six more months, John sported a cast as the healing process continued. As each old cast was replaced with a new one, there were telltale signs that the leg was getting stronger. Even today, John's leg carries the scars, with a definite *Z*-shape to his shin bone. Because of the severity of the fracture, his "bad" leg is one and one-half inches shorter than his "good" one.

Nothing to Fear but Fear Itself

To be useful as a soldier in the army, one requirement is

the ability to run up and down a hill carrying a gun. Although John was finally able to walk, he couldn't run. The army agreed that he would need to recuperate for some time, but they would keep him on active duty and find something else for him to do.

There was another possibility: medical retirement. But John wasn't ready to consider that option. Not yet, anyway. First there was the matter of convincing himself he could still fly.

With his leg shortened by the Z-shaped bone, his foot slightly twisted, and less than 100 percent movement in the affected leg, flying seemed out of the question. Even if he *could* fly again, would he *want* to? Or would the crash have left a permanent fear of flying? John had to find out for himself.

"The very day after the cast was removed for the last time, I went to the airport where a friend had a small plane. Although my leg was stiff and had no strength from being in a cast for 21 months, I was excited to find I could still fly a plane. And I was not afraid!" One obstacle had fallen.

Ready or Not, Here I Come

It was decided that John would accept a medical retirement from the army. By doing this he could be discharged before his full 20 years were up and still receive most of his retirement benefits.

John turned his sights toward MAF and becoming a full-time missionary pilot. He learned there was an opening in Irian Jaya for someone with John's background and training. John was ready and willing to volunteer. But MAF felt he needed some additional training with the special equipment and techniques of jungle aviation. To his disappointment, the door to Irian Jaya slammed shut.

"I didn't like it at first. I was eager to get on with the task, ready to leave for Irian Jaya immediately. When they told me I couldn't go because they didn't feel I was ready, that was hard to take. Now, with the wisdom of 20/20 hindsight, I can see their point of view. From the standpoint of a pilot I was well qualified. But emotionally, there were wounds that still hadn't healed. I can see now I really wasn't as prepared as I thought I was. But at the time, I was pretty upset about the whole thing."

Tuna Fish, Anyone?

"Upset" is perhaps an understatement. John was disappointed enough to tell MAF he had decided to pursue another career.

John located a job in San Diego flying a helicopter off a tuna boat. It was the fulfillment of an earlier dream—a lucrative job flying for a commercial company. But in a matter of weeks, John discovered—if you'll pardon the pun—that the job stank! The pictures on the walls, the talk around the tables— none of it was conducive to spiritual growth!

"Although I was on the boat two weeks, it only took a few hours to realize this was not my kind of world. But I had a problem. I had signed a contract with the owner. We were to leave in two days, and be at sea for three months. I prayed like crazy and determined to quit if the manager would let me out of the contract. I was sure he would blow his stack, reminding me in very salty language that we had an agreement, one I would have to keep whether I liked it or not."

But God had gone before him and paved the way. "After I told the manager I would like to break the contract, he said—to my utter amazement—that he was sure he could work it out with another pilot and it would be fine if I wanted to quit."

John thanked the manager, grabbed his equipment, and made straight for a phone to call Shirley and tell her he was on his way home.

Hello, Is Pilot John Home?

The drive from San Diego to their home in Los Angeles took about two and a half hours. When John arrived, Shirley greeted him with some electrifying news. Since *his* telephone call, there had been another—this one from *MAF*—inviting John to take an assignment in Kenya, East Africa. An urgent need existed for someone to take over the management of a large multinational project involving MAF. John's qualifications exactly fit the need. Would he be interested?

Would he! John immediately phoned MAF headquarters and told them God was obviously putting together all the pieces of a puzzle. He would be delighted to take the Africa assignment.

And that was how—*at age 39*, with a wife, teenage daughter, and Z-shaped shin bone—John Kelley became involved as a missionary in Nairobi, Kenya.

Nairobi is home base for MAF's African operations. From there, MAF pilots transport missionary personnel and supplies not only in Kenya, but also throughout the Sudan, Tanzania, Uganda, and Zaire. John explains his ministry this way: "In many African countries, the roads are impassable much of the time. And when the roads are in good repair, often the vehicles aren't. So the missionaries and nationals depend on us to get supplies to them.

"For example, we ferry all the medical supplies for two

hospitals in Zaire. Those two hospitals provide the only medical services available for *6 million people*. Every aspirin, every bandage, every surgical instrument must be flown in by MAF plane.

"Now we have a most unusual and unique opportunity. We are working in cooperation with World Vision in the nation of Mozambique, a country that is closed to traditional missionary work. But the nation is in desperate need. They have been stricken by a severe drought. The government has given permission for World Vision to come to the aid of its people in agriculture and water projects and to distribute food in the hardest hit areas. We fly people, equipment, materials and food stuffs into the country. Otherwise, it would be impossible to get the people and the food together because of the poor condition of the roads."

After serving for a term in Nairobi with MAF, John is now the Director of Maintenance, Recruiting and Purchasing for a new organization called Air Serv. They are doing relief and development work in several African countries, particularly the Sudan, Mozambique and Ethiopia, flying personnel and equipment into these areas that are in such desperate need.

A Final Word

A remarkable life story indeed! And new chapters are being written in John Kelley's missionary career each day. Remember, he's still only in his 40s!

But before you conclude, "I could never do what John did," consider this closing thought from John's own lips:

"I know that many times people seem to put missionaries on a pedestal, as if they were some kind of superspecial breed of people. But I know that God can use just plain, ordinary people as well, because that's all I am."

For a pilot who enjoys flying with his head in the clouds, that sounds like a man with both feet firmly planted on the ground.

7
FROM MISSILES TO MISSIONS
Bob and Judi Waymire

Adventure and excitement. You don't have to go to the North Pole or the African continent to discover them. Sometimes they can be found in the most unexpected places. Ask Bob and Judi Waymire. They began the biggest adventure of their lives at the breakfast table.

Bob enjoyed a high-paying, responsible position as director of a missile task force. The future looked bright. And yet, for weeks he and Judi had been wrestling with the decision to leave the aerospace industry and launch a new career as full-time missionaries.

Could they have possibly misread the tugging they felt in their hearts? Were they being foolish or was this a divinely ordered step of faith? Together they bowed in prayer and committed themselves to God for whatever the future held.

They didn't have long to wait. Just then, the postman arrived with the day's mail and the confirmation from God they had sought. But we're getting ahead of the story.

———————

Missiles, not missions, were Bob's early passion in life. After a stint in the navy during the Korean War, Bob found himself studying law days and working nights at Northrop Aviation's missile division. His studies and job ended suddenly when his father fell on a construction job in Nevada and broke both arms. Bob joined his uncle to help complete the project.

When his family no longer needed him Bob returned to the West Coast. He was married now and hired on with the missile division at Lockheed. The salary was large, and so was the challenge. For the next few years Bob was heavily involved in research and development for the Polaris missile guidance system. Bob made frequent trips to Cape Kennedy (now Cape Canaveral) to oversee the loading and testing of the new missile. He missed only one of the first 12 firings, and that so he could be on hand for the birth of his first daughter.

A Mile High in Hog Heaven

In 1962, Bob decided it was time to leave Lockheed and pursue a life-long dream. He'd been raising a few calves as a hobby. Now he would become a real rancher on a thousand-acre cattle ranch in Colorado's Rocky Mountains. "I was a mile high in hog heaven," Bob remembers.

Bob's heaven was to last only three years. One evening he walked into the strangely quiet ranch house. A note from his wife said she had taken the children and left him for a Kansas cattle buyer. It was four days before Christmas.

From the Stockade to Lockheed

The ranch had lost its appeal. Deeply depressed and frequently contemplating suicide, Bob soon returned to his old job at Lockheed and tried to forget the dream that had turned into a nightmare. The intense pressure of a new project, the Poseidon missile, helped fill the deep void he felt.

At first Bob stood the stress of his new situation well. An occasional drink seemed to help, but before long he was drinking more and coping less. "Here I was, personal assistant to the director of the Poseidon project," Bob recalls, "and I couldn't even find my way home in the evening." Sympathetic friends helped Bob move into an apartment near the plant with another Lockheed man.

All this time, Bob's secretary Ann was faithfully witnessing. It wasn't easy. Bob insisted—sometimes kindly, sometimes rudely—that the way he ran his life was his own business. One Friday evening after work, Ann and Bob were walking to their cars. "Bob, it's one thing to throw away your life," Ann said, venting her pent-up frustration, "but don't you know you're throwing away the lives of your kids, too?"

"Don't talk to me like that," Bob bristled.

But Ann persisted. She knew he remained in contact with his children and cared deeply about them. "No, Bob, you're still their father. Those kids love and respect you. Do you want them to end up like you? Turn to my friend Jesus. He'll give you the desires of your heart."

Clean and Free Inside

They talked further, and finally Bob knelt down in the parking lot and prayed. "Actually," Bob confesses, "she pulled me down. But no matter. I meant that prayer with all my heart."

That Friday evening Bob went home sober for the first

time in months. The next morning his roommate brought the usual whiskey and beer Bob used to "get going." "Thanks," Bob said, "I won't be needing that any more. I'm a new man." The next day he moved to his own apartment.

Bob took the New Testament Ann had given him and went to a field nearby, an open tomato patch. There he spent the entire day reading the Bible and talking with God. The following day was Sunday, and Bob went to church with Ann. During the invitation he responded by making a public confession of faith in the new Lord of his life.

More Threads in a Divine Tapestry

Bob's decision to switch from missiles to missions was the culmination of a gradual, natural process. He stayed on at Lockheed, grew in his faith, and music began to fill spare hours as he unlimbered a long-neglected trumpet. Then the music led to romance. Bob married his accompanist, Judi, and little by little, God began to bring missions into their lives.

That same year, a Billy Graham crusade was scheduled to come to Oakland, California. Bob attended one of the preliminary organizing meetings, held at the home office of Overseas Crusades (OC) in Palo Alto. For several weeks, he traveled regularly to the OC office, and there became friends with many of the missionaries.

A report from OC missionary Luis Palau challenged Bob's faith. Luis needed $25,000 for a film that would multiply his ministry. "Well," Bob responded, "let's raise the money!" Two hundred people came to a banquet, and the money was pledged.

The pull toward missions was becoming irresistible.

For the first time, Bob and Judi began to discuss the possibility of resigning from Lockheed and becoming full-time missionaries.

Confirmation from On High

It was not to be an easy decision. They would be leaving a secure, high-paying job for a life of spiritual rigors and financial uncertainty. Sitting at the breakfast table, united in purpose and prayer, they began the biggest adventure of their lives. And God promptly confirmed their step of faith in two tangible ways.

The postman arrived with a letter from the Internal Revenue Service—a $95 refund from an overpayment of taxes *two years earlier!*. Bob commented, "It was as if God were saying, 'I can make things happen that you haven't dreamed of.' The amount of the check was small, but the timing was exactly right to encourage us and let us know that God would provide for us and take care of us as we followed Him."

The second confirmation came from Bob's boss at Lockheed, who was not a Christian. Bob expected him to ridicule the notion of joining a mission group. As he scanned Bob's letter of resignation, Bob was surprised to hear these words: "Waymire, what took you so long? God be with you."

And what was Judi thinking of this sudden turn of events? "Well, it might sound dull and unexciting. But I had no struggle at all. I had been praying before I ever met Bob that whoever the man in my life was to be, he would be a man who desired to please God and follow Him. Bob wanted to do precisely that. So when he started talking about missions, I was immediately interested."

Up until this time, missions had never seemed like a

"live option" in Judi's family plans. "When I was growing up, and before I met and married Bob, I had never really thought about personally becoming a missionary, or being married to one. But when Bob started getting involved with the Luis Palau team, I was behind him 100 percent. And later, I was completely in favor of his leaving Lockheed to begin working full-time with Overseas Crusades."

Charting the World of the Church

Once the decision was made, Bob saw even more clearly how years of training at Lockheed had uniquely prepared him for ministry with OC. As director of his own missile task force, Bob had used PERT (Performance Evaluation Review Technique) charts to control an enormously complex managerial task. Now this tool borrowed from industry was put to work to plan a major evangelistic thrust in Latin America. Precrusade activities, training, radio broadcasts, TV coverage and follow-up were all catalogued, organized and monitored on a time line.

Bob's horizons continued to expand as he worked on the new *Global Church Growth Bulletin*. He soon found himself on his way to the Philippines to do church growth research. Using his findings, he co-authored *A Church Growth Survey Handbook* with Peter Wagner at Fuller Seminary. This pioneer work is now used in mission study centers around the world and has been translated into several foreign languages.

Bringing the Globe into Sharper Focus

Today, Bob researches with a mission task force whose assignment is to collect and arrange data on evangelical missions in every country of the world. This global data

Anyone who really wants to be used by God will discover that God has no age limit or mandatory retirement age. I believe the older a person grows, the greater grows his or her potential for service."

—Bob Waymire

base is now being transformed into computer graphics. At the touch of a key, detailed color maps flash on the TV monitor. With a few more key strokes, people groups and mission agencies are identified, along with the growth rates of their churches."

"For the first time, missionaries on the field will be able to see geographically and statistically what has been accomplished and what remains to be done," Bob says, explaining his brainchild. "Our goal is nothing less than to implement a vision of worldwide evangelism."

Judging from Bob's accomplishments so far and his ability to complete complex tasks, no one's going to be surprised when he completes this latest project—and probably in record time.

Looking Backward, Looking Forward

When asked if he had any regrets about changing careers in mid-life, Bob responded, "I have absolutely no regrets about becoming a full-time missionary."

That's not to say Bob's life has been free from discouragements, particularly in the earlier years. "The disappointments," Bob explains, "were usually the result of my unreasonable or false expectations. Not recognizing the good hand of the Lord. Not giving God time to work out His plan. Trying to uncover the *why* behind every *what* and becoming confused and frustrated in the process."

An essential part of spiritual growth is what the Bible calls "dying to self," and Bob was not spared that part of the maturing process. "I found myself relying on my past dealings in the secular world, thinking I could apply those experiences to my new ministry. I could see ways to do things better and quicker, and wondered how Christians ever got anything done using their inefficient methods. I felt that I was eminently qualified and that God was so smart to have chosen me for His team."

Then two verses of Scripture came alive in Bob's life: "Unless a grain of wheat falls into the earth and dies, it remains by itself alone" (John 12:24, *NASB*), and "Not that we are adequate in ourselves to consider anything as coming from ourselves, but our adequacy is from God" (2 Cor. 3:5, *NASB*).

For Bob Waymire, the dying process began as he prayed, "Lord, you made me. You have a perfect plan for my life. Help me to have the peace and patience to enter into it."

A Final Word

"Anyone who really wants to be used by God," Bob reflects, "will discover that God has no age limit or mandatory retirement age. I believe the older a person grows, the greater grows his or her potential for service. God didn't create us mature, nor does He expect us to become mature overnight. The Bible talks a lot about grey hairs and the wisdom which only comes with age."

Potent words from a man whose potential for God's service seems to grow with each passing year!

8

FOLLOWING GOD ON A WING AND A PRAYER

Bill and Doris Waldrop

"Grounded." The one word every fighter pilot dreads.

After 17 years of flying as one of the air force's top pilots in the Far East—and with more than 200 combat missions to his credit—"grounded" was a word Bill Waldrop hardly expected to hear. But the doctor had left no room to argue. Suddenly, the man whose greatest thrill was maneuvering a sleek jet at a thousand miles an hour found himself restricted to "flying a desk" for the rest of his military career.

But while tunnel vision was keeping Bill out of the cockpit of a plane, it was setting him free to see vast new horizons in the service of his Lord. God was about to show him that the air force has no corner on exciting opportunities in the "wild blue yonder."

What could be better than an appointment to West Point Military Academy? According to young Bill Waldrop, *nothing!* According to young Bill's father—a respected civil lawyer—*everything!* He had been grooming Bill to take over a successful law practice.

Bill's parents were devoted Christians who saw to it that their son attended church faithfully. "I guess I really can't remember a time when I didn't believe in Jesus Christ," Bill recalls. "And through the years I've tested that by asking myself if I really knew the Lord as a small child. I concluded that I did because when I thought of dying, my first response was that I would immediately go to be with Jesus. I did know Him in my heart."

West Point continued to beckon, and after a year in prep school Bill received his appointment. For the next two years the influence of the church faded from Bill's life. He had little interest or encouragement in pursuing spiritual things. Drinking with the other cadets became a regular part of Bill's routine.

But while trying to find acceptance in the bottom of a bottle, Bill noticed another group of cadets with a different motivation. They met early each morning for Bible study and prayer—a serious commitment that meant getting up at 5:00 A.M.

"The thing that impressed me most was that these were some of the top cadets, both academically and athletically. They demonstrated a commitment to Jesus Christ that I had never seen before. I had never met contemporaries who seemed to have life all together as these cadets did. They were totally sold out to Jesus Christ. They could look you straight in the eye and tell you their whole motivation for life was to honor Jesus in whatever they did."

As a result of this group's influence, Bill took a bold new step in his own walk with God. "I knew I was a Christian, but in reality I was only a convert, not a committed, growing disciple. I made my decision then and there to become an earnest follower of Christ." Bill began to strengthen that new resolve by getting up before dawn for prayer, meditation and Bible study. Once a week he met with other laymen, and together they encouraged one another in the role and responsibilities of discipleship.

Off We Go into the Wild Blue Yonder

After graduation from West Point, Bill chose to make his military career in the air force as a fighter pilot. Flight training was followed by a tour of duty in Okinawa, where Bill took several giant steps in his spiritual pilgrimage.

Bob Boardman, an ex-marine with combat experience on Okinawa and now a missionary with the Navigators, took Bill under his wing and began to meet regularly with him for prayer and Bible study. It was there on Okinawa that Bill saw the mission field firsthand. Up until then missions had been a once-a-year event in his home church— slides, songs and an offering. But now Bill saw missionaries and mission work "up close and personal," and what he saw made him hungry to learn more.

A group called the Officers Christian Fellowship (OCF) sponsored a conference in Japan, and Bill was invited to attend. There he met a young New Jersey school teacher named Doris, and soon their romance was flying high. With Doris teaching in Japan and Bill reassigned to Texas, their courtship at first had to be carried on long distance by letters. When Doris returned home to New Jersey the following year, Bill continued to court her—at the speed of sound! "On weekends I would fly a trainer from Texas to New Jersey, getting in my flying hours and also my dating hours." They were married later that year.

During their remaining years in the air force, Bill and Doris were active in the Officers Christian Fellowship as well as the base chapel programs where they lived. From time to time someone would suggest the possibility of Bill resigning from the air force and working full-time with the Fellowship. But Bill was enjoying flying too much to take that thought seriously.

The Vietnam War was heating up, and Bill received his orders to ship out. He flew over 200 combat missions, received the Distinguished Flying Cross and eight other air medals, and represented his wing in the Far East Weaponry Meet, where he competed against the top pilots in the United States Air Force.

While Bill was sharpening his flying skills, he was also sharpening his knowledge of other countries in Asia. A growing vision for the world and a burden for the lost were the result. He recalled something he had seen in Doris's home church. "One of the things that impressed me in the front of the sanctuary was a pair of big globes representing the two hemispheres of the world. On those globes were lights representing all the missionaries the church supported.

"Now, although I didn't like the reason for my being in the Orient, it did give me an opportunity to visit several countries and see firsthand many missionaries and ministries. I was exposed to other cultures and religions. I could see graphically the tremendous lost condition of people without Christ, and the power of the gospel to transform them."

A Wider Perspective Through Tunnel Vision

But Bill's life was about to veer off course, or so it seemed to him. Nothing is more precious to a jet-fighter pilot than his eyesight. When a routine flight physical turned up Bill's loss of peripheral vision and depth perception, overnight his flying days were over. Bill's dreams of becoming a wing commander were dashed.

The leaders of the Officers Christian Fellowship talked to Bill more earnestly about retiring at the 20-year mark—only three years away—and joining their staff full-time. This would be a natural transition for Bill, following on the heels of his extensive involvement with the Fellowship over the years.

But there was still the tug of the military for Bill to contend with. If he did stay on, he would be up for promotion to full colonel. Though his flying days were finished, the thought of another promotion, greater pay and increased responsibility were all very appealing.

Slipping into the Will of God

Bill was weighing carefully his decision about retirement. The leaders of the Fellowship were praying that Bill would feel God's call to join them. The thought of another promotion was pulling Bill in another direction. It was all so confusing. What Bill really needed was some time alone to seek God's mind.

Bill and his family took a weekend trip out of state before returning to base on Sunday evening. It was bitterly cold, and freshly fallen snow had made the footing treacherous. Bill tried to get everything out of the trunk in one trip. With bags and boxes piled high, and slick snow beneath him, he slipped—and tumbled to the ground in a heap. When Bill tried to stand up, his back wouldn't return to its original position. Monday morning he shuffled into the doctor's office, still shaped like a question mark. After a brief examination, the doctor announced, "A week in bed for you doing absolutely nothing."

A divinely ordered prescription! Bill's constant companions during that week were his Bible, legal pad and pen. Gradually, he began to sense what God was saying about the new direction of his life's work.

When the week was over, so too was Bill's search. As he listed the pros and cons of each choice, studied God's Word for guidance and prayed for understanding and wisdom, God answered in an unmistakable way. At last, the decision was made: upon completing his 20 years, Bill would retire from the air force and begin working with OCF. In order to be as prepared as possible, Bill felt the next step was seminary training.

Doris Waldrop had been well prepared for yet another family move. "Being in the military will do that for you!" she recalls. "You move often. We had been doing that every year or two since we had been married. So the thought of packing again and moving to a new location wasn't all that traumatic for me. However, I was concerned about something else. The military had been more than our *life*—it was also our *ministry*. We had both been heavily involved with the Officers Fellowship. And now I would have to regear my whole life to being the wife of a student. I wasn't sure how all that was going to work out."

But work out it did, for *at age 42* with two teenage boys and two decades of air force experience—Bill Waldrop traveled with his wife Doris to Boston where he enrolled and later graduated from Gordon-Conwell Seminary.

While Bill was taking a full-course load, he was also overseeing the OCF ministry at West Point, Annapolis and the Coast Guard academies on weekends. During the summer he worked full-time with OCF in their conference ministry and also found time to do some writing.

While at seminary, two men had a profound and lasting impact on Bill's life. One was faculty member Dr. J.

I had learned early in my Christian life that my overall objective as a Christian was to become like Christ. I realize more than ever before that God wants to shape my life and in the process He will use me, if I allow Him, in whatever work and ministry He has for me."

—Bill Waldrop

Christy Wilson, former missionary in Afghanistan until the government burned his church to the ground. Dr. Wilson increased Bill's burden for missions around the world. The other man God used to mark Bill's life was Dr. Harold J. Ockenga, then pastor of the Park Street Church in Boston. From him, Bill saw how missions could and, indeed, must become a vital part of the local church.

For Doris, the years in Massachusetts were both busy and fulfilling. "Seminary was an exciting time for both of us. We were both looking forward to working with the Officers Fellowship full-time and realized how important this phase of preparation would be. In addition to filling the roles of wife and mother, I found time to join the seminary wives' organization, serving as president of that group."

The Road Turns South

Shortly after graduation, Bill received a long-distance phone call from Atlanta, Georgia. A new church was starting on the south side of town. About 75 people were meeting weekly. Would Bill consider accepting the call to become their first pastor?

"I was completely flabbergasted," Bill recalls. "I told the caller I had never been a pastor before and had never really contemplated becoming one."

"Well, we've never been a church before either," the caller responded, "so why don't you come and we'll learn together?"

Just the kind of challenge fighter pilots thrive on! But Bill was not ready to commit himself—not yet. "All I can say at this point is that I'll pray about it. I'll let you know in six weeks what I believe God wants me to do."

Was God saying something? *Should* Bill really give this invitation from out of the blue serious consideration?

Could God be leading once again in a totally new direction? Bill's whole background had been in the military. He had prepared himself by going to seminary, expecting to have a ministry exclusively with military personnel and their families. The thought of becoming a pastor had never crossed his mind—until now. In fact, when he did think about it, he quickly concluded the job of a pastor must be the toughest assignment on earth!

One overarching life goal guided his thoughts: "Getting to know my Lord better, then serving Him *wherever* and being willing to do *whatever* He wants me to do." That life goal guided Bill as unerringly as a lighthouse: "Where will I become a more Christlike man?" Bill reflects, "I had learned early in my Christian life that my overall objective as a Christian was to become like Christ. I realize more than ever before that God wants to shape my life and in the process He will use me, if I allow Him, in whatever work and ministry He has for me."

During the six weeks that followed, Bill spent many hours alone with his Lord, his Bible and his ever-present pad and pen. But he also spent long hours together with Doris. She had several questions that needed to be answered as well. "It would be a brand new adventure for us," Doris remembers. "We really had never thought about being in the pastorate. Our whole married life had revolved around the military. We were comfortable with that type of people. But a pastorate? We had seemingly no preparation for that kind of task. And I had no earthly idea what my role as pastor's wife would involve. I knew what an *air force officer's wife* should do, but not a *minister's wife*. And there really weren't any courses in seminary to prepare the wife for that sort of role!"

But in spite of her doubts, Doris remained positive and supportive toward Bill. "Whatever you think God wants you to do, whatever He is leading you to do, will be fine with me because I am your helpmeet, and I know God can lead you."

After weeks of waiting on the Lord, Bill accepted the pastorate of the new church. And that August, he and his family moved to Atlanta to pastor the Grace Evangelical Church. Bill comments now, with a hearty chuckle, "All my suspicions were confirmed. The pastorate *is* the toughest job in the world!"

Cultivating Missions in the Local Church

Bill's teaching gift was now being utilized to challenge and inspire missions interest and involvement in his church. His expository sermons were rich with biblical truth and practical application. Under God's hand of blessing the church quadrupled in size.

In Bill's first year as pastor, the church's missions giving was a modest $3,500. The next year it jumped to $16,000, and the following year to $50,000. Currently the missions budget is in excess of $100,000—not bad for a "flock" of 300 members!

But in 1985, God had another road for Bill and Doris to travel, a direction every bit as unique as the one that lead them into the pastorate.

Bill had been involved with the Association of Church Missions Committees (ACMC) from its inception several years earlier. Because of Bill's deep interest in missions in his own church, ACMC had invited him to speak on missions in other churches and ACMC-sponsored seminars. Bill could articulate the worldwide cause of missions, combining personal overseas observation with practical pastoral experience.

Recognizing the ideal "fit" of Bill's background and abilities to the task of challenging local churches with the unfinished task of world evangelization, ACMC approached Bill about joining them full-time in an at-large capacity. His assignment: helping local congregations to begin their own missions programs. Years in the pastorate, a heart for missions and a successful program of local missions involvement. The pieces seemed to fit. Could this all have been a prelude to even bigger things to come? The thought was certainly intriguing.

Meanwhile, Doris was entertaining her own thoughts on the matter. "Where would I fit into this new ACMC ministry? It would basically be Bill's ministry. I had shared Bill's commitment to the ministry. So I was still committed to being part of whatever he felt God was saying to him. But all my life I've been a pretty active and involved person. I'm not content doing nothing. Earlier in our marriage, the children were, in a sense, my ministry. But now the nest is empty. Bill and I have really been a team throughout the years, and I just wanted to be sure my gifts would be used to enhance his ministry."

That "enhancing" ministry is starting to blossom, as Doris works with ministers' wives. Recently on a mission trip with Bill to Romania, Doris enjoyed an extensive teaching ministry among pastors' wives and missionaries as well.

The psalmist tells us, "Delight thyself also in the Lord; and he shall give thee the desires of thine heart" (Ps. 37:4, *KJV*). From the Officers Christian Fellowship to Grace Evangelical Church to the Association of Church Missions Committees, Bill and Doris have delighted themselves in the Lord and discovered the delight of being used in His service.

Bill Waldrop, wanting to become a more Christlike man, was willing to follow God's direction in his life.

At age 39, a fighter pilot.

At age 42, a seminary student.

At age 45, a pastor.

At age 55, a missionary-at-large.

Too old to serve?

"Never!" Bill responds with a cadet's enthusiasm. "Not when you and God are in the same cockpit together."

9
GOD'S MARINE IN SOUTH AFRICA
Jerry and Gladys Stowers

His full name is Earnest Marine Stowers. His father was a marine during World War I, fighting in Europe. When Earnest was born, his dad, proud of his marine heritage, tagged his son with the middle name. "I'm just glad," Earnest reflects, "that Dad wasn't in the Coast Guard."

But no one calls him Earnest or Marine. It's always been Jerry. When he was born, his aunt exclaimed, "Look at that little Jerry"—the German's nickname for a marine—which might explain Jerry's early confusion over exactly *what* his name was. "My diploma from high school reads 'Earnest Marine Jerry Stowers.' I didn't even know my real name until I graduated from high school. Everyone just called me Jerry."

So let's call him Jerry, like everyone else. And let's find out how Jerry the *soldier* became Jerry the *student* and eventually Jerry the *printer* thousands of miles from his native Georgia.

World War II was in full swing when Jerry graduated from high school. Like so many of his classmates he enlisted

right out of school. Before Jerry left for boot camp he
promised his high school sweetheart Gladys that as soon
as the war was over, they would be married.

From boot camp Jerry shipped out to Guadalcanal for
mop-up operations. Later, he participated in the initial
marine amphibious assault on Guam, and a few weeks
later joined in the fight for Iwo Jima. Three of the hottest
battlefields in the Pacific theater, and yet Jerry made it
through without a scratch.

His love for Gladys deepened during those 30 months
of separation. Three weeks after his discharge, they were
married. Jerry found a job at a large printing company in
Atlanta, little knowing how greatly God would multiply his
talents over the next 30 years.

A Good Guy, but Not Good Enough

During Jerry's early years, his parents took him to church
regularly and passed on sound moral values. "My mother
taught me her basic philosophy in a song: 'One, two,
three, four, five, six, seven, all good children go to
heaven.' And I tried to live like a good boy. I wasn't
involved in the typical 'worldly' things. I would not drink or
smoke. I didn't curse or run around. Even during my time
in the marines, I maintained high moral standards. Of
course, my testimony now is that if I had been killed in battle, I would have been a nondrinking, nonsmoking, non-
cursing sinner in hell. But at the time I was sincerely trying to live a good moral life."

Someone's Knocking at My Door

A few years after Jerry and Gladys were married, a lady
knocked at their door and offered to teach them the Bible.

They invited her in and for several weeks spent time together. "What she was teaching was confusing, though," Jerry admits. "We had both grown up in the church and were attending church at the time. Although we weren't converted then, we felt what she was teaching was in conflict with what we thought we believed. Something didn't quite ring true. We didn't know much about the Bible, so we really didn't know *what* to believe."

Jerry contacted a friend who offered to come and teach them more about God's Word. "For the first time in my life I was confronted with truth that could change my life. As I learned Bible doctrine, beginning with the doctrine of man, I realized how far away from God I really was. I learned about the separation that exists between holy God and sinful man, and that a right relationship with God begins with who He is, not with what I have done. In May 1951, when I invited Christ into my life, everything changed!"

That change is reflected in the names of Jerry's three children. "You can tell from their names exactly when we were saved. Greg, our oldest, was named for Gregory Peck. Marilyn, our second, for—well, you guessed it. And after our conversion, our third, Deborah, came along."

Boot Camp Revisited

Jerry and Gladys fell in love with the Word of God and the God of the Word. They saw how much they needed to grow spiritually. And they started reaching out to others with their faith. Gladys began to visit the women's section of the county jail to teach the Bible and saw many come to Christ. Jerry went to the juvenile court each month and shared his newfound faith with the young people. Bible classes, Sunday School classes—their ministry began to grow and bear much fruit. Jerry was enjoying his work as a printer. What more could this dynamic, dedicated couple ask for? What more indeed?

And After Retirement, What Then?

Twenty-one years came and went with Jerry working at the same printing company. Then one day Jerry glanced across the printshop floor at a fellow worker. The man was 65 years old and only days away from retirement. The thought came to Jerry, "In a few more years, that fellow will be me.

"Here I was, driving back and forth to work, putting food on the table for my wife and three children. But apart from my work at the church, I was doing nothing of real significance with my life. As I thought some more, I found myself saying, 'You know quite a bit about the Bible. Maybe the Lord could use you someplace else for the rest of your life, instead of just marking time here at the printing company.'"

Oh, By the Way . . .

Gladys picks up the story from there. "That very afternoon I attended a ladies' Bible study. At the conclusion we were praying as we always did—for our families, husbands, unsaved friends, the sick, unspoken requests. Nothing unusual or out of the ordinary. But when we had finished praying, I looked at my friends and said matter-of-factly, 'By the way, Jerry and I are going to the mission field. I guess I'd better tell Jerry when he gets home.'"

Gladys met him at the door and announced, "Jerry, I need to talk with you about something the Lord has been saying to me today." They made their way to the backyard and sat down together on a swing.

"You know," Gladys continued, "for a long time we've talked about going all over the world and preaching the gospel. And we've been supporting missionaries who are doing exactly that. But the Lord has been talking to me today through His Word."

Gladys then shared with Jerry several verses the Lord had used to speak to her heart. One in particular was Romans 12:11 (*NKJV*), "Fervent in spirit, serving the Lord." At that point in their lives, Jerry and Gladys could scarcely be described as fervent. They were serving the Lord, to be sure, but giving Him only their tired hours on the weekend, reserving their best hours for their work and private lives.

Gladys then posed a question: "Jerry, do you suppose the Lord has something more for us than what we're doing now?"

"Normally," Jerry said, "if Gladys had told me, 'Let's eat supper and then go shopping,' I would have said, 'No thanks, I'm not interested.' But here she was saying that maybe we should sell our house and leave America. And I heard myself saying, 'Sure, I think that's what we should do!' It had to be the work of the Lord in my heart."

The date was August 3, just days before Jerry's forty-second birthday.

Mature Words from a Minor

Jerry and Gladys weren't quite sure how to proceed. Initially, they thought about selling their house, buying a mobile trailer and traveling around the country looking for struggling congregations in need of revival.

Sensing the need for some timely Christian counsel,

they attended a conference in the beautiful mountains of North Carolina. There they spoke to Dr. Stephen Olford and shared with him God's call and guidance in their lives. That night Dr. Olford announced from the pulpit that there was a couple in attendance who wanted to go to the mission field. After the service, Jerry and Gladys were surrounded by interested people.

One man said he knew of a ministry in Africa which suited them perfectly. Another suggested they should go to Bible school. Jerry's reaction was anything but enthusiastic. "I already knew quite a bit about the Bible, and besides, I hadn't been to school in almost 25 years." But in spite of his objections, the idea intrigued him.

Their son, Greg, was a third-year student at Columbia Bible College. When he heard what his Mom and Dad were considering, Greg gave them some mature counsel of his own: "I'm proud of you both. All I ask is that you don't let this drop, but that you keep pursuing it." Fatherly advice from a son!

Pursuing a goal is one thing; achieving it is something else. And in the Stowers' case, the obstacles loomed tall: an ex-marine in his 40s, with one son in Bible college and a daughter about to enroll. If Jerry and Gladys applied, that would make *four members of the same family in Bible college at the same time!*

And suppose they *did* enroll and were accepted and graduated together. What then? Printing was all Jerry knew. But what good is *that* on the mission field?

Then there was the family house. Should the Stowers sell it or keep it in the event things didn't work out? At least that way, they would have something to fall back on. Jerry could always come back to Atlanta and start his own printing business.

Questions tumbled one upon another. Questions that

We didn't stop. We kept pursuing what we deeply believed God wanted us to do and had already confirmed to us in several ways."

—Jerry and Gladys Stowers

had to be answered. And one by one, the answers that
emerged seemed to point in the same direction.

Pack the U-Haul, Y'All

At last, the decision was made: sell the house, pack the
truck, move to Columbia, South Carolina and enroll in
Bible college. The Stowers family was going to school!

"We had decided to sell our house as a step of commitment to the Lord. We felt we really needed to make that
definite break and not leave anything to hold us back."

The FOR SALE sign went up, and Jerry and Gladys
went next door to explain to their neighbors why they
were leaving Atlanta. Incredibly, their neighbor said, "You
know, Jerry, my wife and I have been talking about the fact
that you were probably going to Africa as missionaries."
Incredible—because up to that point, Jerry had not said a
word to anyone about their plans.

A few days later, one of Greg's friends brought a book
by the house for them to read. Its title: *Trailblazing in
Africa*.

In the midst of packing for the big move, the phone
rang. It was Columbia calling. After Gladys hung up, she
told Jerry, "That was the college. They say we've been
accepted. Wasn't that nice of them to call us personally and
tell us that?"

Jerry explains: "We were so naive, we didn't even realize you *had* to be accepted. We were just planning to go.
Now with our acceptance in hand, we were on our way."

The Sunday night before they were due to leave,
Gladys gave a testimony in their church. She shared about
God's leading them to Bible college and their determina-
tion to go whether their house sold or not. After the service, one of the deacons came up and asked Jerry, "Do you

mean your house hasn't sold yet, and you're just picking up and leaving?"

"Well, yes, that's right. We're packed and ready to leave first thing tomorrow."

"I would like to buy your house. I haven't seen it, but I know the area. I'll buy it. What are you asking for it?" Jerry explained to him what they had hoped to get out of the house.

"Fine, I'll arrange to get the money to you."

The stage was now set: U-Haul packed and pointed toward Columbia; three children, the youngest in high school; and *four family members* enrolled in Bible college!

During the next two years, the Stowers immersed themselves in the study of the Bible and missions. To help make ends meet, Jerry worked several hours a day on the maintenance crew at school. As the family studied for classes, they spent long hours thinking and praying about what they would do and where they would go after graduation. They talked to many missionaries about the kinds of ministry opportunities overseas. Not everything they heard was encouraging.

"We talked to the deputation secretary of one mission organization who told us, in as many words, to forget it and go back home. We were discouraged, but it didn't slow us down because we knew that God had called us and placed us where we were. We decided that if one little road block like that could stop us, then maybe we shouldn't go. But we didn't stop. We kept pursuing what we deeply believed God wanted us to do and had already confirmed to us in several ways."

The Pieces Begin to Fit

Sometime later they talked to Dr. Bob Foster of the Africa

Evangelical Fellowship (AEF). They explained what they felt the Lord was saying to them and asked what counsel he would give. "Interestingly enough," Dr. Foster commented, "I've just returned from a trip to the southern part of Africa. One of the greatest needs we have right now is for someone to take over the printing work in South Africa. It's going well, but the missionary in charge is having serious physical problems. We're looking for someone to replace him immediately."

Jerry's ears perked up. Printing? Africa?

Dr. Foster encouraged the Stowers to fill out an application. "That will give us a chance to see if we like you, and give you a chance to see if you like us."

They were accepted as candidates with AEF and began raising their support. A short time later they accompanied the president of Columbia Bible College, Dr. Robert McQuilken, to a mission conference in Chattanooga, Tennessee. Jerry was asked to speak in a Sunday School class, sharing their proposed ministry in Africa. The class became a part of the Stowers' support team. Soon full support was in hand. At age 43, Jerry and his family were headed to South Africa as first-term missionaries.

Keep the Presses Rolling

Today, Jerry's printshop operates at full speed, supplying materials for AEF's 9,000 users of Bible correspondence courses in six foreign languages. In addition, Jerry publishes a series of booklets on basic Christian doctrine which is widely used in South African churches.

More than 600,000 men labor in the gold mines of South Africa. Many of these miners commute from neighboring African nations, and provide a unique ministry opportunity. Several groups of Christians circulate among them each day passing out tracts printed on Jerry's press, visiting the miners when they are in the hospital, showing Christian films and holding public meetings which attract as many as 3,000 interested participants.

"The ultimate goal, of course," Jerry explains, "is to see these miners converted and then see them take the gospel with them when they return to their own countries and homes. In fact, our church in Botswana was started by a miner who was saved in South Africa. He went back to his country, started sharing the gospel and, as a result, a church was planted. We now have 11 missionaries working with our churches. But it all started with one miner converted in South Africa. Last year 2,208 miners came to know Christ as Savior through our work. My part is simply to print the literature that is used."

I've Gotta Be Me

Shortly after the Stowers arrived in Africa, the need arose for someone to teach a small group Bible study for women. Gladys eagerly stepped into the gap. Since then, scores of women have come to Christ through Gladys's ministry in Bible study groups and "Free to Be Me" seminars. As many as 400 women meet to hear seminars and messages on timely subjects of special interest to women. Gladys has trained about a dozen African women to lead these retreats. The conferences have now spread to include neighboring countries as well. Jerry prints the workbooks and materials and duplicates cassette tapes of each session.

Postscript from a Printer

Jerry and Gladys's contagious enthusiasm for missions has been caught by their children. Greg and his family are missionaries in France; Marilyn and her family, in Spain; Deborah and her husband are in business in South Africa.

Does Jerry plan to retire in a few years and come back home to Atlanta? "No," he replied without hesitation. "I don't think that will ever happen. We fully expect to work and live out our lives here in South Africa.

"Recently, Gladys and I visited our former home on Gardenia Lane in Atlanta. We looked at our house and then at each other and agreed that we wouldn't want to relocate to Atlanta for anything in the world. There has not been one regret."

Earnest words from the heart of Earnest Marine Stowers!

10

FROM THE MILITARY TO
THE MINISTRY

Forest and Coleen Pierce

He has the bearing of a soldier: trim, solid, piercing eyes, gentle strength. And he comes by it honestly, having spent over 25 years as an officer in the United States Army, retiring as a full colonel.

But Colonel Pierce might well have been General Pierce, and therein lies a story. For the man whose life-long ambition was to rise to the top in his chosen profession, resigned in order to enlist in the service of his other Commander in Chief.

How did a 25-year military man come to such a life-changing decision? The answer is as fascinating as the man. _____

The sounds of war rumbled through Southeast Asia, and Forest Pierce received orders to assume command of a battalion in Vietnam. Leaving family and home is never easy, especially in time of war. Forest recalls, "I was going to an area where I really didn't know what was going on, and I wasn't sure what the next year would bring."

That tour of duty was the perfect "classroom" for God to teach Forest lessons that would mark him for life.

Forest had joined the Army after graduation from Kansas State University, where he later received a master's degree as well. After a tour of duty in Alaska and completion of the Command and General Staff College, Forest was assigned to duty in the Philippines. While there he saw firsthand the work of missions, the urgent need for more harvesters, and the desperate plight of the Filipinos without Christ.

The next stop for Forest was Fort Leavenworth, Kansas. There he became active in the chapel programs and Officers' Christian Fellowship. And there he met Dr. Bob Smith and observed a dedication of life and purpose that he had previously never known. "Dr. Bob," as he was known, would become an important counselor and mentor in Forest's life in the years to come.

But first Forest had to survive his tour of duty in Vietnam.

Nagging Questions on the Battlefield

Forest's unit had lost 270 men in the previous three days. Two weeks earlier, the unit commander had been killed. It was time to move out and evacuate the battlefield—fast.

"As I traveled over Vietnam I could see the purposelessness of life apart from God," Forest recalls. "So many had no hope, only fear of death. I could see there must be something more to human existence than just death itself. And if there *was* more, what assurance was there that these people had had an opportunity to hear about it? When you come face-to-face with death and destruction, you begin thinking more seriously and deeply than ever before."

But the most difficult struggle for Forest concerned the will of God in all of this. One of the unpleasant tasks Forest faced was positioning his men on the battlefield, especially when it became obvious the fighting would be intense and the chance of survival slim. This forced him to think deeply about the meaning of life. "Why is it that the youngest and brightest of my men seem to be the ones who always get killed?" The question haunted him and seemed to defy an answer.

Returning to the United States, Forest faced yet another question: "Why did I make it safely home without being killed or injured, while so many of my buddies didn't?" He finally resolved the question by resting in the thought that God must have something important for him to do—something that would become clearer in the months just ahead.

General Pierce, I Presume?

Forest was being moved along in his army career on the "live track" for high promotion. After returning from Vietnam he was assigned to the Personnel Department in Washington, then to the Naval War College and later to the Armed Forces Staff College. But a new dimension was being added to his life.

As he became more active in Bible study and prayer groups, Forest found himself enjoying the study of God's Word more than his preparations for college lectures. This prompted more serious thoughts about his future. "Should I stay in the army, with an almost certain promotion to general? Or should I resign from the army and perhaps think about going to seminary?" To a military officer, promotion to the rank of general represents a lifelong ambition. "General Forest Pierce" would have a satisfying ring and provide the finishing touch to an enviable career.

Forest began to talk—and listen—to his trusted Christian friends, seeking counsel for his future. "Dr.

Bob," who had come to speak at a series of Bible study sessions, offered his counsel as well: "There are sacrifices that must be made in the service of the Lord. You have a family. You need to think about educating your children. And you will be in school, too, if you go to seminary. You'll need to maintain a home. Some sacrifices will have to be made."

In recalling that counsel, Forest remarks, "It was not pessimistic. It was not hilariously optimistic. But it was very realistic, from the standpoint that all of these priorities impinge—and rightly so—on anyone who is making the decision to go into the ministry."

Resigned to Resignation

Forest began assessing his life and background to see if there were indicators from the Lord about the future course he should take. He deeply loved the study and application of biblical truth; he demonstrated the gifts of pastor and teacher; he had learned many skills and principles from his military career that would be invaluable in the ministry.

Then there was the family. Coleen remembers, "I was looking forward to retirement. We already had a nice travel trailer and had been making our plans to go visit all these nice places and do all the things we had been dreaming about.

"But on the other hand, we had also been praying that our lives would be fully committed to the Lord. The thought of getting out of the military and going to seminary wasn't really that difficult for me. I had seen it coming for a while so it wasn't a big surprise.

"The military life we had lived for 25 years really prepared me for this new move in our lives. Actually, there was a little anxiety about it. I had had a year of solid anxiety already when Forest was in Vietnam. I never knew where he was during that entire time. I only knew he was somewhere in a forward artillery position. So I would read the newspapers and learn where he probably was by the location of the heaviest ground fighting.

"That year was very difficult. Being a child of God, I had the peace that only He could give. But being human, it was a difficult and anxious year. That experience brought home to me the very practical and necessary truth about trusting God and leaning only on Him. So anything after that, even going to seminary at our age, was really no problem at all."

While Forest was wrestling with the future course of his career, Uncle Sam stepped in to change the military retirement regulations. Ironically, if Forest had chosen to remain in the army, he actually would have received less retirement in the long run. Once again, God was using circumstances to teach Forest important lessons in relying upon Him.

At last the decision was made: Forest would resign from the army and apply to seminary.

Several of Forest's fellow officers urged him to change his mind. One in particular, an admiral, expressed great satisfaction with Forest's work as an officer and teacher. At Forest's retirement party, that same admiral called him and Coleen into his office. They talked for over an hour, with the admiral saying how much he admired Forest's decision and that he was considering a similar career change sometime in the future!

Grey Hairs in the Graduating Class

And so, *at age 46*, Forest Pierce enrolled at Denver Conservative Baptist Seminary. The confirmation of wise counsel, coupled with a deep inner peace, encouraged Forest that he was on the right track of God's will. "Never before had I experienced such peace as I did after making my decision. In fact, I had some strange anxiety, believe it or not, to actually get to seminary and get on with it. I really wanted to study the Word so I could find some answers for myself. I sensed a deep inner calm that I had made the right decision."

Forest's fellow seminary students readily accepted him as their peer, though with his grey hair he looked more like a grandfather than a graduate student. Dr. Vernon Grounds, president of Denver's Conservative Baptist Theological Seminary, opened the first day of class by saying, "I can see that the average age of our class has been raised measureably."

The academics of seminary life proved a special challenge to Forest. "When I started, I had to put myself back 25 years to the time when I was studying for my master's. And when you start taking those Greek courses, you find yourself second-guessing your decisions. I found myself wondering if I could do it academically. But after the first semester, I knew that the academic life of seminary was essentially no different than what I had come to expect in Kansas."

The army had done a wonderful job of preparing Forest for the rigors of seminary. "In the courses that required a lot of writing, I just applied the same principles to write a paper on theology that I had used in the army to write 'staff studies' on military subjects. I was conditioned in the army to look at the right, left and center, then to put forth the arguments that would lead to a proper conclusion. I simply applied those same principles to my seminary courses."

As an officer I was trained in the whole area of management techniques which I used for years in the army. And now I've discovered a great need for management skills in the local church as well: to delegate jobs, to set goals, to develop the various stages of a ministry, to be able to get a diverse group of people working together harmoniously."

—Forest Pierce

Coleen was a vital part of his seminary experience as well. She, like many a wife of a seminary student, received her P.H.T. (Putting Hubby Through) diploma. In addition to keeping the family wardrobe in shape with the help of Stretch-and-Sew courses, she helped out in the political campaign of a close friend.

"But my main contribution was as chief typist. It always seemed that on big term papers, Forest would finish about three o'clock in the morning. Then he would wake me up and I would type like crazy, finishing just in time for him to take the paper to class that morning."

Unexpected Harvest in the Home

While Forest was wrestling with his decision to enter seminary, his father—who was not a Christian—had difficulty accepting his son's career change. He couldn't understand why Forest would want to give up all the security and prestige of being a high-ranking military officer, to go into the ministry.

One afternoon, as Forest answered his father's questions and objections about the Bible and the Christian life, Forest had the joy of seeing his father bow his head to accept Jesus Christ as Savior. "I believe I would gladly have gone through seminary if for no other reason than to answer my father's questions and see him come to know the Lord. That made all the hard work well worthwhile."

A New Challenge for an Old Chief

Coming from a management position in the military into the full-time Christian ministry, Forest had much to learn about the concept of servanthood. "Moving from the military as a full colonel, with a staff of officers and enlisted men under me doing my bidding, to the role of servant seeking to make others successful—well, it was something I had to deal with.

"The Colorado church I pastored was a new one, just beginning. We met in a school building where everything had to be set up each Sunday. I ended up doing a lot of the 'set up' myself, plus many other chores as the only person on the pastoral staff. That might have been the hardest thing I've ever had to do. Not the physical labor, of course, but my attitude toward being a servant."

Forest was beginning to learn what Jesus meant when He said that "the Son of Man did not come to be served, but to serve" (Matt. 20:28, *NKJV*).

After serving in this new church for a few years, Forest accepted a position on the staff of a large church in Colorado Springs.

For men and women who, like Forest, go into vocational Christian work late in life, God doesn't waste the lessons, experiences and training gained over the years. "As an officer I was trained in the whole area of management techniques which I used for years in the army. And now I've discovered a great need for management skills in the local church as well: to delegate jobs, to set goals, to develop the various stages of a ministry, to be able to get a diverse group of people working together harmoniously. In my preaching I have over 40 years of personal experience to draw upon. This helps me in using illustrations that speak to people right where they are."

A Final Word

The apostle Paul likens devoted Christians to good soldiers of the faith. That means there is armor to put on and military principles to obey. Forest Pierce has a clear head-start on most of us when he listens to Paul's words through the "grid" of 25 years of military experience. And now he is using all that experience to lead a growing church in Colorado.

Too old to change careers? Too old to attend seminary? Too old to exchange a life in the *military* for a life in the *ministry* or on the *mission field*?

Take it from Forest Pierce: You're *never* too old to enlist with the Lord!

Section Three
FROM THE ATHLETIC WORLD

11

FAST BREAK TO THE PHILIPPINES

Paul and Nancy Neumann

A 1983 issue of *Sports Digest* contains a trivia question about basketball: "Who was involved in the trade that sent Wilt Chamberlain from the San Francisco Warriors to the Philadelphia 76ers?"

The correct answer is the subject of this chapter.

For many years Paul Neumann's life not only revolved *around* basketball—it *was* basketball.

Twice he was selected team captain at Stanford University, was named Northern California Player of the Year, was selected for the UPI All-American and Converse All-American teams, was top scorer his senior year, ranked in the top 10 all-time scorers in Stanford University history and capped off a sparkling collegiate career by being inducted into the Stanford Hall of Fame.

But ask Paul today for the highlight of his college days, and he will take you back to a day during his sophomore year: not a championship game or awards banquet, but the quiet occasion when God spoke to him about making a total commitment of his life to "go into all the world" (Mark 16:15, *NKJV*).

"Venture for Victory." A funny name perhaps for a basketball team, but an appropriate title for the turning point
in the life of basketball great Paul Neumann.

Because of Paul's athletic ability, he was invited to join
one of Overseas Crusades' evangelistic sports teams that
would be touring the Orient the summer after his graduation from Stanford. The experience gave Paul a firsthand
glimpse of many different cultures. But more important,
Paul saw the pagan religions that hold millions in darkness
and fear—and how lives can be transformed by the power
of the gospel.

The sights and sounds of the Orient made an indelible
impression upon Paul. But when he returned to California,
basketball soon returned to center court in his life. Post-
poning plans to play professional basketball, Paul com-
pleted a master's degree in secondary education in preparation for a coaching career. In the process, he still found
time to play on an Amateur Athletic Union (AAU) team,
tour Russia with the U.S.A. Select team and be named to
the AAU All-American team.

With his master's degree in hand, Paul turned professional, playing first for the Syracuse Nationals. Two years
later the franchise was sold and became the Philadelphia
76ers. There Paul toiled for three years before being
traded to the San Francisco Warriors. In the last year of
Paul's professional career, his team won the Western Division championship, beat the Los Angeles Lakers and
Atlanta Hawks in the playoffs and faced his old team, the
Philadelphia 76ers, in the championship series.

Is There Really Life after Basketball?

Even the most illustrious basketball career cannot last forever, and Paul began to wonder what might fill the void once his basketball days were over. "I would look up in the stands, see all those people who had come to watch us play, and wonder if I could do something more than just entertain the crowds."

Paul retired from professional basketball and returned to his alma mater as an assistant coach. Although he was having winning seasons at Stanford, he couldn't shake an unsettling, searching feeling. Slowly, a new course for his life began to take shape.

Paul recalled the many missionaries who had stayed in his family's home and spoken at his father's church. "I particularly remember hearing a missionary from Africa tell a story about how he saved an official's life by fighting off a lion in the bush of Africa. That really impressed my young mind at the time."

The "Venture for Victory" trip to the Orient had broken down many of Paul's preconceived notions about mission work. "Up to that point, my concept of a missionary was the old Frank Buck image—you know, pith helmet, big black Bible, the old stereotype. And I wanted no part of it."

Paul began reading books on missions that stimulated his thinking and challenged him to consider again his life calling. The summer of 1969 marked the turning point in Paul's career. With his wife Nancy, he attended the Overseas Crusades missions week at Mt. Hermon Conference Center. The speaker asked a question that split Paul's heart: "When are you going to start being the person you promised God you would be?"

Shaken, Paul thought back to the time during his sophomore year when he told God, "Here's my life." The speaker was right; when *would* he make good on that promise?

Over-trained and Under-qualified

That night a growing interest in missions was born. Paul decided to make himself available for overseas service, although he wasn't sure he had what it takes. In Paul's own words, "I was over 30, had four children and no formal Bible training. My whole life and training were in the arena of basketball. I was sure that would eliminate me from missions."

There were other factors as well, other "barriers" God had to break down in the life of His willing, if somewhat wary servant. During Paul's years in professional basketball, his salary had been substantial and his life-style far from austere. Materialism was a very real force to be reckoned with, as Paul honestly admits. "Even though I was a Christian, and a Sunday School teacher at that, I had pretty much swallowed the world's system of values."

Nancy Neumann had her own battles to fight. "We had pretty much 'arrived' in the way the world measures success. Although Paul's salary as a professional basketball player was nothing like the salaries today, for that time it was pretty handsome. We had a nice home and all that goes with it. But we were beginning to discover it wasn't all that important."

Several years earlier, Nancy remembers a commitment she had made. "Actually, before we were married, we both had committed ourselves to go to the mission field. We had sort of felt that one day we would be pursuing mission work overseas someplace. We were committed to that. But I guess somehow it was moved to the back of our minds as other things crowded in."

But more than anything, one question continued to haunt Paul: "When are you going to start being the person you promised God you would be?" At last, he sought out

Dr. Dick Hillis, president of Overseas Crusades (OC), about becoming a missionary.

"I really didn't understand much about missions at that time," Paul admits. "I just knew God wanted us involved in some way. Nancy and I determined that if God would open the door, we would walk through it. There were no bright lights flashing, no visions from Macedonia, no loud voices to catch our attention. We just said, 'Okay, God, it's time to do it.' And He seemed to agree!"

Nancy adds: "God had apparently been working in the kids' hearts, too. Danny and Cindy were too young to really understand, of course. But Eric came home from camp that same summer talking about how much fun it would be to go to the mission field. It was neat to have that little confirmation from the Lord."

Counsel to the Contrary

As Paul and Nancy began to share with close friends what God was doing in their lives, many expressed amazement that Paul would leave his successful coaching career to become a missionary. Some of their Christian friends actually tried to talk them out of the idea. "Why are you going overseas when there is such a great need here at home?" "You are so successful in what you're doing. Why waste all that talent, training and education on people who won't appreciate you anyway?" "They have their own religion. Why confuse them by adding another?"

But the staggering imbalance of Christian workers in America when compared to overseas—94 percent of all Christian workers laboring among only 6 percent of the world's population—was the only argument Paul needed to hear. "True, there are needs in the United States. And the spiritual need is the same, whether here or abroad. But there is one big difference. While the need is the same, the opportunity to meet that need is not. So I simply say, 'Why not?' And if not me, then who? And if not now, then when?"

Fast Break to the Mission Field

Dick Hillis suggested the next step would be a year of graduate Bible study at Multnomah School of the Bible in Portland, Oregon. But time was short, and only a miracle could pave the way for the Neumanns to enroll for the fall term. It was late August, well past the application deadline. Paul would have to resign his coaching job, find a buyer or renter for the house in San Jose and locate suitable accommodations in Portland for his growing family of six—all in a matter of days.

In times of major change, the enemy becomes particularly active, accusing, tempting, discouraging. Paul made an appointment to see the head coach at Stanford to inform him of his decision. But when Paul arrived, the secretary told him the coach would not be able to see him until the next day. That night Paul found a letter in the mail from the athletic director at Stanford—very complimentary of his work, and announcing a handsome raise for the coming year. For a moment, Paul wavered.

"I had to ask myself if I was really making the right decision. The drop in salary from being a pro player to becoming a coach had been a shock. Now I would really be joining a new 'salary bracket' by becoming a faith missionary. In a few short years my four children would have education expenses. If I stayed at Stanford, that would be no problem. If I left, well . . . . "

The next morning Paul talked with the head coach and

*Our life is Christ in us,
using us for His purpose.
It's a great feeling when you're
starting to become the person
God had in mind when He
created you in the first place."*

—Paul Neumann

explained his decision. The coach, who was not a Christian, could not begin to comprehend what Paul was planning to do or why, but he wished Paul well. The miracle had begun.

Although the deadline for enrolling had come and gone, Multnomah made an exception in Paul's case. Within a week, a Christian family was found to rent the Neumann's house in San Jose. By applying so late, the Neumanns learned that all the school housing was already full. But a friend's uncle just happened to have a house for rent only seven blocks from the school. Within three weeks Paul had applied to Overseas Crusades, resigned his job, rented his house, moved his family to Portland, and begun studies at Multnomah.

Paul's Three Missionary Journeys

With his classwork behind him, Paul journeyed with his family to their first field assignment: Indonesia.

Nancy remembers that first assignment with mixed feelings. Honest feelings. Wife-and-mother type feelings. "I suppose I really hadn't prepared properly for Indonesia. I guess I was looking at things through rose-colored glasses. I was living in the spiritual clouds someplace and rather naively thought everything and everybody, including myself, would be just perfect."

But the mission field has a way of injecting a generous dose of reality into such feelings. Sights, sounds, smells, unreadable words, unintelligible sounds—all these can flood in upon you when you first arrive on the field. Nancy continues her honest comments: "We hadn't been there but a few days when I began saying to myself, 'Paul, what have you *done* to me?' My first reaction was: 'Oh no, you mean I've got to live in *this* place—for *four years?*' I felt like I had been dropped off the end of the world."

Why was Nancy reacting like that? "Many reasons—and good ones! The filth all around was unbelievable. There are many canals that wind through the capital city of Djakarta. They are so dirty, you can virtually walk on the water. Then there was the lack of privacy. People were seemingly everywhere. I had to retreat to the bedroom and close the door in order to feel like I was alone. I found myself despising the very people I had come to show the love of God to."

Not a very good way to begin a missionary career. Was victory over all this quick to win and easy to maintain? The pain is gone now, but Nancy recalls those difficult early days. "I spent the first six months in various stages of depression. I cried a lot. I retreated to the bedroom and tried to read to take my mind off things. I didn't want to go outside. I didn't want to talk to people. About all I really wanted to do was go back to the good ole U.S. of A., where it was clean, where I understood the language, and where the electricity worked 24 hours a day."

After six months, things began to change. God was dealing with Nancy's attitudes, and the chastening was not always gentle. To Nancy's credit, she responded obediently. "I finally saw that I had to do something positive. It was a conscious effort on my part. I finally, consciously, decided one day that 'enough was enough.' I had to make a choice—to decide whether I was going to have a *bad* experience in Indonesia or a *good* one. With the Lord's prodding and encouragement, I decided it was going to be a good, positive experience."

The cure for Nancy's depression began to take hold. "I started digging in. I got out of my house. I began to learn some of the Indonesian language. In short, I started thinking and doing what I should have been thinking and doing right from the start. God began helping me turn things around. Believe it or not, I started to enjoy being in Indonesia."

Three years later with the sports program of OC expanding rapidly, Paul was asked to return to the States to coordinate the teams being sent out. Then back to the field once again, this time to the Philippines, where sports ministries, Bible conferences, and a newly organized church growth research center in Manila have kept Paul on a perpetual "fast break" for the past 12 years.

In the Philippines, Paul introduced the six-hour Bible survey seminars called "Walk Thru the Old and New Testament" to excited crowds from Manila to Mindanao. "It's thrilling to see the response to this survey of God's Word," Paul reports. "As you teach, you can see the lights turn on in the minds of people as they see the Bible come alive as never before. We're seeing many first-time decisions for Christ as a result of the seminars."

Now, after having spent several years in Asia, Paul and Nancy have added a new continent to their passport and another language to their brain. Overseas Crusades recently opened up ministry in Argentina. Paul and Nancy were asked to join that team to help train the pastors and church leaders of that rapidly growing church there. Paul remarked about all these changes: "Let's see. *Salamat pagi* was Indonesian. Then *Magandang umaga* was Filipino. And now *Buenas dias* is Spanish. Oh well, only 5,000 more languages to go. I might make it!"

A Final Word from Paul, the 20th-century Missionary

"One of the verses God has used in my life is Paul's statement in Philippians 1:6 (*NIV*): 'Being confident of this, that he who began a good work in you will carry it on to completion.'

"One of our biggest concerns was for our four children and their education. But God provided a terrific mission school for them in Manila and has made it possible for all of them to attend college.

"Naturally, there have also been some discouragements and disappointments. It was disappointing, for example, when some of our close Christian friends didn't seem to understand why we wanted to be involved in missions. That was discouraging. And occasionally I wonder where I would be now if I had stayed in coaching. That's normal for anyone, I suppose. But God has been faithful, as the verse says, 'to carry on his work' in us and through us.

"Another of Paul's verses that God has used in my life is 2 Corinthians 4:7 (*NIV*): 'We have this treasure in jars of clay to show that this all-surpassing power is from God and not from us.' That is what our life is all about. Our life is Christ in us, using us for His purpose.

"It's a great feeling when you're starting to become the person God had in mind when He created you in the first place." For Paul and Nancy Neumann, new chapters in that becoming process are still being written.

Section Four

PUTTING IT TO WORK

12

NOW IT'S YOUR TURN

Imagine you are sitting in a comfortable chair in a large living room. Seated around you are the 11 couples you have just read about, men and women ranging in age from mid-40 to mid-70.

You have been considering some type of full-time involvement in Christian work. But you're not sure if it is just a passing notion, a moment of unbridled enthusiasm— or if there is some substance to the thought.

You're experiencing a wide range of emotions: confusion, anxiety, exhilaration, doubt. There are questions you would like to ask, pieces of advice you'd like to gather, and this is your opportunity.

Sit back. Relax. Find a notepad and pencil. Get ready to ask the knotty questions that have been troubling you. But before you begin, remember one important thing.

No magic formula exists for determining the will of God in an individual's life. Talk to 10 people, and you're likely to get 10 different answers, maybe even 12. But there are time-tested principles waiting to be gleaned from the pages of God's Word and the experiences of others who have walked with God. The path into full-time Christian service is well-worn, and the questions frequently raised fall into clearly identifiable patterns. Are you ready to ask *your* questions?

———————

QUESTION: Aside from the obvious importance of Bible reading and prayer, where should I begin in thinking about full-time Christian service? What questions should I ask myself?

Forest Pierce: I would say you need to ask yourself, "Why am I thinking about the possibility of leaving my current job? Is it because I'm unsuccessful in it? Or because the grass looks greener somewhere else? Or am I running from some problem I don't want to deal with? If so, don't get into Christian work. If ego is your motive for change, don't change."

Dick Harris: Maybe the question that Dr. D. James Kennedy asked me when I was considering going to seminary is apropos here: "Is there anything *else* I can possibly do?" If so, that's probably what I *should* be doing.

Charlie Spicer: I would suggest another thought. You need to be involved where you are now, particularly in the matter of sharing your faith. If you don't have a heart for the lost in your own circle of acquaintanc es, crossing an ocean won't change that. You'll find it's harder, not easier, to develop a burden for someone overseas that you've never met. The best place to begin being a missionary is in your local church.

No magic formula exists for determining the will of God in an individual's life. Talk to 10 people, and you're likely to get 10 different answers, maybe even 12. But there are time-tested principles waiting to be gleaned from the pages of God's Word and the experiences of others who have walked with God."

—Keith Brown/John H. Hoover

Paul Neumann : Let me follow that line of thought by suggesting another question to ask yourself, "Do I know what my spiritual gifts are, and am I taking steps to cultivate them?" Begin using them now in your local church. Crossing an ocean will never compensate for inadequate preparation at home.

QUESTION: How do I test my motives for wanting to go into full-time Christian work? How can I be sure I'm moving in that direction for the right reasons?

Forest Pierce: You need to ask yourself and settle the issue once and for all, "What is the limit of sacrifice I'm willing to make in order to serve God?"

Charlie Spicer: I would add another dimension to that. The whole idea of what to do with your personal assets is very important, and there is no easy answer to it. Do you sell everything you own, cash in your investments and give it all away? Do you sell some and keep the rest? Or do you keep it all and put it to work in the ministry of the Lord? Basically, it's an individual matter, and something you'll need to resolve very carefully and prayerfully.

John Kyle: There is another area of potential tension. If you are entering Christian work from a background in the business world, and especially from a management position, you need to be prepared to struggle with lines of authority. When the leader you work under or alongside of lacks administrative skills and training, the result can be tension, friction and frustration.

Bob Waymire: After I joined a Christian organization, I wondered at times how anything ever got done. I quickly saw how things could be handled more efficiently, and it was difficult at first for me to work with others who didn't see things from my perspective.

Shirley Kelley: You need to be prepared for misunderstanding, even by members of your own family. Many people told us we were wasting our lives. Some of our family actually became bitter because we were leaving the States and wouldn't be around for "family things." Expect that, and it won't knock you off balance.

QUESTION: I can think of more good reasons why I *shouldn't* enter Christian work than reasons why I *should*. I don't really have that much to offer the Lord. After all, I've never been to Bible college or seminary, I'm getting up in years, my kids are still in school, I owe quite a bit of money, and my boss would never allow me to leave my present job. What would you suggest?

Dick Harris: Don't worry if you're 30, 40, 50 or however old you may be. Don't let age be a factor. It certainly isn't in God's eyes.

Charlie Spicer: Don't allow a lack of formal Bible training to discourage you. It's certainly wonderful if God opens that door, and by all means take advantage of all the Bible training you can get. But never forget, there are many areas of ministry where you can serve with little or no formal Bible training.

Arthur Lown: Never allow a handicap to prevent you from pursuing a dream. My blindness has been an inconvenience at times, but never a hindrance. Don't forget that God reserves the right to use anyone in His service, regardless of his or her handicap.

Paul Neumann: In my case, I felt it was important because of my ministry with pastors to get some formal Bible training. The year I spent in graduate studies at Multnomah School of the Bible has proven invaluable time after time on the mission field.

Dick Harris: Believing that God was calling me into the pastoral ministry, I found seminary training both necessary and mandatory (the Presbyterian Church in America requires it).

Jerry Stowers: You can trust God to work things out, even when things look unworkable. If you have a God-given compulsion that you should do something full-time, don't be worried about the money or selling your house or breaking old ties or lack of education. God has a way of taking care of all those things if we'll just lean on Him.

Author's Note: The question of Bible college, seminary or other formal Bible training is an individual decision that should be made in consultation with the particular denomination or organization you intend to represent.

QUESTION: How has your employment background been utilized in your full-time Christian work? Were those just "wasted years" or, looking back, can you now see a purpose for the jobs you held in the secular job market?

Arthur Lown: God is the Master at conserving the resources in the lives of His children. Yesterday's training becomes grist for tomorrow's ministry. My ministry in Jesus' name to the blind of the Philippines was simply the extension of my ministry to the blind students of Atlanta.

Dick Harris: Don't look at your past experience as wasted time. I not only know what the Bible says, but I can illustrate many of its principles from my 45 years of life in the secular business community. To me, it's a tremendous advantage not to have gone straight from college into seminary.

———————

QUESTION: Let's suppose I've worked through all of your suggestions, and now I'm quite confident God is saying something to me about changing careers and entering full-time Christian service. What then?

Bob Waymire: Three key ingredients in successful preparation for the mission field or pastorate are time, time and still more time. Don't grow impatient when God's timetable seems to be different from yours.

John Kelley: I certainly had to learn that the hard way. Trying to do God's will in your own way and in your own time can only lead to frustration. My life is Exhibit A that God's timing is always best.

Howard Jones: Don't try to force open those doors or knock them down, even if they are pursuits you would especially like to follow. Frequently, God will open a door you are totally unaware exists. When He does, don't question His leading, even if it doesn't seem to make good earthly sense at the time. Once you have committed everything to Him, you have nothing to lose by being obedient to Him.

Jerry Stowers: Take one step at a time. Think of it as driving a car at night. The headlights shine about 200 yards down the road and no farther. But when you have traveled those 200 yards, you can see another 200 yards and so on.

QUESTION: I'm available for God's service, all right. But how can I really know when God is calling me or directing me?

Howard Jones: Don't expect God to take you by the hand and lead you this way or that. God has given you a mind and He expects you to use it. Once you have made your unconditional commitment to Him, expect God's Spirit to work in your spirit and mind to give you direction.

Charlie Spicer: That's right on target. We need to use good common sense. Don't be carried away with an emotional response. That's like trying to base your salvation on your feelings. It doesn't work. God has given us wisdom—common sense—and He expects us to use it in determining His will.

Howard Jones: Let me add another thought. Don't be disappointed when God's will comes quietly, rather than dramatically. Some people look for a cyclone or earthquake to accompany God's leading. Occasionally God does use a Damascus Road experience in the life of one of His children. But not often. More commonly, He uses a still, small voice—and that means listening attentively if you're going to hear it.

QUESTION: Then where does God's will fit into all of this? How do I know that what I'm planning to do is really His desire?

Dick Harris: You need to have an understanding of the Word of God. That means serious Bible study with the aim of becoming grounded in that book.

Bob Waymire: You cannot impart what you do not possess. It's not enough to become enamored with the missionary cause. You must master and, in turn, be mastered by God's Word.

John Kyle: When you study God's Word, you discover the program and passion of God to reach the world. You need to understand missions from God's perspective.

Charlie Spicer: The Bible was very important in our decision-making process. Through personal Bible study and pastoral preaching of the Word, I saw the Bible come into focus to provide direction and confirmation.

QUESTION: And what about the role of prayer?

Doris Waldrop: In our family's experience we have had several weeks of deep, concentrated prayer at important transition times as we sought the Lord's will.

Howard Jones: Pray often, "Lord, I'm willing to go anywhere," and be sure you mean it. No ifs, ands or buts.

Dick Harris: Exercise your prayer life daily. Everyone I talk to in the ministry or missions says the same thing. Without prayer, you can't do a thing.

Charlie Spicer: Getting alone with the Lord and letting Him deal with you provides the inner confirmation that is so essential. Prayer helps verify the inner thoughts of the heart.

Bob Waymire: Surround yourself with a circle of praying men and women. Cultivate the habit of prayer in your own life. There is a direct correlation between intimacy in prayer and effectiveness in ministry.

QUESTION: Apart from the Bible and prayer, which we have already mentioned, what other signposts did God use along the way to guide you into His place of service for you?

Lois Kyle: I would say an important signpost was the counsel we received from others; our minister, other Christians. Don't overlook the advice of Spirit-led laymen and laywomen. The key here, of course, is that those whom you seek out *are* Spirit-led, mature Christians who have a deep walk with God.

Doris Waldrop: I would amen that. You definitely need to seek counsel from godly Christian leaders. They can help you be unbiased about your decision. They can give you an objective look at all the factors. You need that perspective and balance.

Charlie Spicer: God often does use the counsel of others—people He brings across your path at just the right time with exactly the right word of counsel you need. The personal experiences and testimonies of others can be a great source of help and encouragement.

Bob Waymire: Right along this same line is the idea of a supportive group of people. You should become involved in a care-share prayer group. A fellowship of supportive Christian friends to whom you can be accountable. Be honest with yourself and transparent with others.

QUESTION: Prayer—Scripture—counsel. Is there anything else?

John Kelley: I would add to the list: circumstances. I believe we can expect circumstances to play a role in God's direction in our lives. For me, the "chance" encounter with an MAF pilot only four days after my conversion, the TV special that just "happened" to be on, the timely missions banquet, even my helicopter crash. All were circumstances along the way which God used to turn my life on just the proper heading to find His will.

Paul Neumann: God certainly used the circumstances of

basketball in my life when I made the trip with the "Venture for Victory" team after my senior year in college. In my mind, it was just a fun excuse to play basketball. Little did I realize at the time how God would use that summer to transform the course of my future career.

QUESTION: It all sounds very positive and upbeat. But isn't there a "downside" to this kind of decision-making? What cautions would you share to help me avoid pitfalls?

Forest Pierce: When changing directions from a lifelong career into the ministry, you can't afford to be doubleminded. Be certain it is a definite decision; no question in your mind that this is what God wants you to do.

Jerry Stowers: Be sure of your calling. Don't try to pattern your call after anyone else's. God reserves the right to work with each of us differently.

Doris Waldrop: Consider your calling very seriously. Be sure that it's not just some whim or fancy or something you merely think you would like to do. I firmly believe a person should remain in the laity until he is definitely led by the Lord to enter the ministry or full-time Christian work of some sort.

QUESTION: It seems so often people hold back or wait. They know God wants them to change directions and become involved in Christian work, but there is a reluctance—a hesitation to make the big decision. Can you suggest some ways to overcome this tendency?

Lois Kyle: Make it a definite project to seek out and find God's will. Don't sit and wait for something to happen. Start taking definite steps. An elder gave me good advice when he told me that a sailboat would not sail unless it is cast away from the dock. He encouraged me to get moving and then allow God to open and close doors along the way. A phrase I've used before is very appropriate: "Many are *willing* to go; but few are *planning* to go." Any action is better than no action. Even if we start in the wrong direction, God can correct us. The important thing is to start taking steps.

Howard Jones: When you know what you should do, don't be slow to do it. There is a time to pray, a time to study God's Word, a time to seek wise counsel. But never confuse *knowing* God's will with *doing* God's will. In Scripture, to know and not to do is as bad as the sin of witchcraft.

QUESTION: Once I have narrowed down the options and all the indicators point to a change, what should I do next? Should I start packing right away or is there more preparation I need?

Arthur Lown: Get actively involved in missions here at home. One of the best ways to get more interested in missions is to start supporting a missionary family.

Charlie Spicer: If at all possible, make a visit to the mission field to see mission life and work firsthand. Talk to missionaries. Find out their needs. Then evaluate your own life and experience to see where there is a need you can help fill.

Bob Waymire: You might consider a short course of study that will expose you to some of the top mission minds, such as the programs offered at the Institute of International Studies at the U.S. Center for World Mission in Pasadena, California.

Paul Neumann: Do some research on the subject of missions. Find out what kind of skills are needed and where. You might also want to consider doing some cross-cultural work right here in the U.S.A. to help prepare you for the future. Begin reading some good missions books. Missionary biographies are also an excellent place to begin. Become knowledgeable about the world in which you live and the world for which Christ died.

QUESTION: Once I have decided God definitely wants me on the mission field, how do I go about selecting which mission organization to join?

Paul Neumann: Get to know several mission organizations. Send for their literature. Study them in order to match your gifts and interests with their particular needs.

Bob Waymire: Do your homework before selecting a mission board under whose authority you will seek to work. Each mission board has a personality all its own, with goals, methods, policies and personnel in keeping with that personality.

Jerry Stowers: Select a mission board as carefully as you would select a marriage partner. Get to know each other thoroughly in order to find out if you can live and work together harmoniously. Once you begin the selection process, you will quickly eliminate several possible choices. But what if you have difficulty narrowing it down to one? Maybe you have three different organizations that all seem to fit you. What should you do then? Probably the best thing would be to start the application process with all three. As the applications are processed, and as you continue to pray and study the Word, God will begin to show you which organization is His choice for you.

God's will and place for you are *just right* for you. It's His desire that you be content wherever He directs you. He's that kind of God. You *can* trust Him with your life.

POSTSCRIPT:
FINDING GOD'S WISDOM FOR
CAREER DECISIONS

Wise counsel from spiritually mature individuals can prove invaluable in determining God's will for your life. As you read the preceding stories, no doubt you noticed the important role counseling played in times of critical decision-making. It's no accident, but rather the obedient response of those intent on doing God's will—nothing more, nothing less, nothing else.

Wise Counsel from Mature Believers

Down through the years, devotional writers have added their own unique lines of timeless counsel—unique in that the words are phrased in the author's own style and filtered through the grid of the author's own experience; timeless in that they are based on the unchanging truths of God's Word.

It is our prayer that this potpourri of selected thoughts will provide just the encouragement, insight and incentive you need to find and follow God's direction for your life.

"There are times when you cannot understand why you cannot do what you want to do. When God brings the blank space, see that you do not fill it in, but wait."

"If we obey God, He will look after those who have been pressed into the consequences of our obedience. We have simply to obey and to leave all consequences with Him."

"Faith never knows where it is being led, but it loves and knows the One Who is leading."[1]

"The truest kind of success from God's perspective can be attained only when we follow His plan rather than our own."

"We really do not know how things are going to turn out ultimately. But God does. He knows us and He knows all the possible consequences of every alternative we can choose. So it makes no sense to choose any plan but His. That is the only one we know will turn out right."

"Finding God's will is not a matter of frantically searching for something hidden. It is following the divine Shepherd, and there is nothing mysterious about that."

"God has maintained an impeccable reputation for faithfully guiding His people, and He isn't about to ruin it now. We can count on His willingness to make His plan known to us. His character requires it."

"While God has the whole journey mapped out ahead of time, He conceives of that journey as a successive series of small steps and that is the way He makes it known to us."

"The issue before us is our willingness to commit our entire future, for time and eternity, to One who offers to lead us only one step at a time, who does not show us His plan beforehand, nor tell us exactly where He is taking us."

"The greatest obstacle to knowing God's plan for our lives is the persistence of our own unbending purposes and preferences."

"The more of the Word we know, the more sound and solid information we can bring to bear on the decisions we need to make."

"If we want only God's will for our lives, whatever the personal sacrifice, and if we open His Word to look for what He has to say rather than for what we want to see, we can expect Him to speak to us through it. He has promised that His Word will be a light to our path."

"Circumstances can be an uncertain guide. While God is in control of every event in our lives, most events can be interpreted in different ways."[2]

"There can never be any guidance contrary to the Word; there will seldom be guidance apart from the Word. Divine guidance must either come through, or in perfect harmony with, the written Word of God. Anything else is not divine guidance."[3]

"Faith is an attitude of will which says, 'Whether I feel that God is there or not, whether I feel He will heed me or not, His Word tells me He hears and answers and I am going to count on that.'"[4]

"Most of us at sometime or other have longed for the quick, neat formula, the easily followed rule of thumb, the overwhelming bolt from the blue. But God normally does not reveal His will in these ways."

"If you have missed God's ideal will for your life, don't panic or despair. Receive His forgiveness through Christ and set your heart to know and do His will where you now find yourself."

"Failures aren't to cripple us; failures are to learn from."

"Take care of your present task."

"Let God engineer your sphere of service as you obey Him. The sphere of service is not nearly so important as the quality of your obedience."

"It is useless to search for God's will if you are unwilling to obey. Often we waste our time in an agony of searching. We kid ourselves. But we do not kid God who knows that we really don't intend to obey."[5]

Wise Counsel from God's Word

King Solomon, the wisest monarch in the Bible, had much to say about the wisdom and safety of godly counsel. His pithy, inspired statements in the book of Proverbs (*NIV*) provide these rich insights:

> For lack of guidance a nation falls, but many advisers make victory sure (11:14).
>
> A wise man listens to advice (12:15).
>
> A prudent man gives thought to his steps (14:15).
>
> Plans fail for lack of counsel, but with many advisers they succeed (15:22).
>
> In his heart a man plans his course, but the Lord determines his steps (16:9).

It is not good to have zeal without knowledge, nor to be hasty and miss the way (19:2).
Make plans by seeking advice (20:18).

Finally, don't overlook the rich lode of other helpful, instructive verses about God's guidance contained in God's Word. And when possible, read each verse in its context, using one or more reputable Bible translations. Study each verse carefully to discover the principles and promises God desires you to know and appropriate. Here is a partial list of Psalms, additional Proverbs and other references to get you started:

Psalm   25:4-5,9-10,12,14;   32:8-10;   40:8;   86:11; 111:10; 119:33-35,97-1 00,104-106,129-130,133; 139:11-12;

Proverbs 2:1-8;   6:20-23;   9:10;   13:10;   19:20-21; 27:17;

Isaiah 8:17; 30:21; 48:17;

Jeremiah 29:11-12.

Notes

1. Oswald Chambers, *My Utmost for His Highest* (New York: Dodd, Mead & Co., 1979), pp. 4,11,79.
2. Richard L. Strauss, *How to Really Know the Will of God* (Wheaton, IL: Tyndale House Publishers, 1979), pp. 13,21,31-32,39,50,57,81,112,127. Used by permission.
3. G. Christian Weiss, *The Perfect Will of God* (Chicago: Moody Press, 1950), p. 80.
4. John Wesley White, *Daring to Draw Near* (Downers Grove, IL: InterVarsity Press, 1977), p. 34.
5. Taken from *You Can Tell the World,* edited by James E. Berney. Copyright 1979 by Inter-Varsity Christian Fellowship of the U.S.A. Used by permission of InterVarsity Press, Downers Grove, IL 60515, pp. 70,72.